ADVENTURES IN T

Historical fiction by
the Young Walter Sc

This collection is © the Young Walter Scott Prize

Copyright in the text reproduced herein remains the property of the individual authors and permission to publish is gratefully acknowledged by the editors.

First published in Great Britain in 2019 by the Young Walter Scott Prize,
Bowhill, Selkirk, Scotland TD7 5ET

www.ywsp.co.uk

All rights reserved.

No part of this publication can be reproduced, stored in a retrieval system or transmitted in any form and by any means, electrical, mechanical, photocopying, recording or otherwise without the prior written permission of the publisher or a licence permitting restricted photocopying. In the United Kingdom, such licenses are issued by The Copyright Licensing Agency. www.cla.co.uk

CONTENTS

	PAGE
About the Young Walter Scott Prize	2
Foreword – Elizabeth Laird, Chair of the Judging Panel	5
Shadow of Hunger by Jenny O'Gorman – winner	7
Dust on the Road by Joseph Burton – winner	13
Transmigration Programme by Helena Baxendale – shortlisted	18
Alien Bouncers by Frankie Browne – shortlisted	23
Little Matron by Catherine Fitzhugh – runner up	28
Lest We Forget by Megan Lintern – shortlisted	33
The Station by Natasha Mirus – runner up	37
The Piper by Andrew Pettigrew – shortlisted	40
The Long Sunset by Jonathan Rhys Clark – shortlisted	47
Deleterious by Elise Swain – shortlisted	53
Vive la Revolution by Jack Tickner – shortlisted	58
*C'est la Vie b*y Tiphaine Tsatsaris – shortlisted	62
Ladybird, Ladybird by Lili Winstanley-Channer – shortlisted	66
The Soldier's Civil War by Lucas Yates – shortlisted	70

About the Young Walter Scott Prize

Waverley by Walter Scott is widely regarded as the world's first historical novel. Set against the backdrop of the Jacobite Rebellion of 1745, it was published, anonymously, in July 1814. That first edition was published in three volumes and the print run of 1000 copies sold out almost immediately. Before long, Walter Scott had an international reputation on a scale few writers have achieved since.

The Walter Scott Prize for Historical Fiction, which will be awarded to its tenth winner in June 2019, celebrates books by some of the world's finest writers in the genre. Its early success inspired its founders, the Duke and Duchess of Buccleuch to extend their support to a new award for young writers, and we're delighted to present this anthology of the winning Young Walter Scott Prize entries in 2018.

The judges – award-winning writers Elizabeth Laird, Eleanor Updale and Ann Weisgarber, Literary Agent Kathryn Ross and the Director of The Young Walter Scott Prize, Alan Caig Wilson – deliberated long and hard before deciding on the winners. Congratulations to all those whose stories were chosen, and many thanks to everybody who entered, and to the many teachers, librarians and parents who supported their entries.

Alongside the Young Walter Scott Prize, a programme of Imagining History workshops is run all over the UK by Alan Caig Wilson. These offer groups of young people a unique opportunity to explore sites and buildings of historical interest, often going behind the scenes to places unseen by the general public. These popular workshops encourage active historical research together with guidance on writing skills.

Information about entering the Young Walter Scott Prize and the Imagining History programme – both open to 11 to 19-year-olds - is on the website.

Both the Walter Scott Prize and the Young Walter Scott Prize are generously supported by the Duke and Duchess of Buccleuch and the Buccleuch Living Heritage Trust.

Young Walter Scott Prize-winners

2015 Joe Bradley and Rosi Byard-Jones

2016 Demelza Mason and Alice Sargent

2017 Leonard Belderson and Miranda Barrett

Walter Scott Prize-winners

2010 *Wolf Hall* by Hilary Mantel

2011 *The Long Song* by Andrea Levy

2012 *On Canaan's Side* by Sebastian Barry

2013 *The Garden of Evening Mists* by Tan Twan Eng

2014 *An Officer and a Spy* by Robert Harris

2015 *The Ten Thousand Things* by John Spurling

2016 *Tightrope* by Simon Mawer

2017 *Days Without End* by Sebastian Barry

2018 *The Gallows Pole* by Benjamin Myers

Foreword – The Chair of the Judges, Young Walter Scott Prize

Enthusiasm, the joy of exploring history, the delight of experimenting with words, and above all the thrill of exercising the imagination - all these leap off the pages of the stories submitted to the Young Walter Scott Prize. It's been a bumper year both for the quantity and quality of the stories submitted, and I've no doubt at all that we'll be hearing from some of these young writers in the years to come.

Elizabeth Laird
June 2019

SHADOW OF HUNGER
Jenny O'Gorman
Edinburgh

Winner of the Young Walter Scott Prize
11 to 15 age-group

'You are going to die.'

At first those words were a charcoal scribble on the soft Irish skies, then they were trodden into the black earth. The men ignored me at first as they scooped up my fine printed letters on their shovels. I was the strange sentence that stood silently in the potato fields, listening to the Gaelic songs drum against the chop and turn of the blighted soil. When I introduced myself to families across the bare table, my greetings were met with anguish. So I just bowed my head in mock sorrow as the children wept. This wasn't the first time Mary-Anne had seen me sit comfortably beside her family at dinner.

"Tis sorry I am, child," was all their Ma could whisper as the watery dribble of broth made a bruise on her daughter's plate.

"T'isn't your fault, Ma."

Pause - you can hear the red sky stirring and boiling as they pray.

As I slip away from the table they begin to chew, mouths like turning oars.

"Amen."

After eating, the two children sit awhile with their mother, watching as she angles calloused fingers towards the open fire. The family are always reminded of me, my pressed suit draped over the stool. Ready for the time I will take them by the hands, and tell them to wave goodbye to Ireland.

****

"Mary-Anne, Séan. Where is your father?" Ma whispers. I try and read her eyes as if we are in a poker game. She shuffles memory cards in the dark, fumbling with her words.

"He's gone, remember?" Séan says uneasily.

"He'll be back soon surely," she concludes firmly, placing her empty hands on the floor. I give Séan a warning look, hoping he won't remind her.

"We'll see him soon Ma," I murmur and stare at the smug shadow standing at the door, displaying the cards it has won.

"Sure and tis worse Ma's gettin'," I agree, once we pass Ó Conghaile's field the next day. The dry grass has the same jaundice that seeped into Pa's face. Séan runs the stick he has found along the cobbled wall. It slips against the humps and hollows, and drags in the clumped moss; a finger along a spine.

"Tis a good stick that's in it!" Séan exclaims, slashing ferns that crowd our path; as we near Father's grave, I make him cease fire in his battle against the plants.

"How'ya Pa?"

Bindweed unbutton themselves into the silent wind, reminding us of the ruffle he gave our hair before bed. Séan scatters a handful of Red Campions, his fallen enemy soldiers.

* * * * * * *

I trudge back along the puddled stench of rotten potato fields with the children.

"They are paler this morning, blurring into a memory."

Another world's sun is touching them, the childish curve of their faces sliding in and out of thin beams of light.

"Not long now, they are almost mine."

"Would you ever stop a while Séan; see the horses?" The young girl sighs, hitching her brother onto the dry stone wall.

* * * * * * *

Farmer Ó Conghaile plods through bracken, ruddy features like a fox cry against the shades of grey. He reaches his thin mare and dying foal. The mother stands still in a sea of barren earth, indifferent or wise to the reality.

"Iosa Críost!" he bellows. "Jesus Christ…"

And I see the shadow cup its hands around the lolling head — the farmer sees it too.

"No!" I scream. But it is too late, Hunger had got the foal, and would kill it eventually. Kinder to end the creature's suffering.

"You'd best be away from here, children, Ireland is no place for young uns. Boat to 'Merica leaves this afternoon."

We watch as he shoulders his battered old flint-lock and dissolves into the early mist.

"I'm not leavin' Pa all alone, we promised we'd look after the land," Séan says crossly.

But the shadow of Hunger walks towards us, hanging mouth moving soundlessly.

"Never mind that, get Ma, we're leaving tonight."

Séan and I try to calm her as she recites fuddled prayers and grips her rosary beads.

"Where is 'Merica?"

"Tis over the sea Ma, there is no hunger there. It'll be a new life for us," I tell her, and hope with everything in me it is true. As we leave our village of Skibbereen, I see the shore wring its hands in worry, until seawater floods over generations of soaked footprints. The boat dries out her lungs in port as the sea rolls over like a whiskered seal.

Battered cleats cupped

In earthy racks of peat.

Sea Stacks lean like

Three legg'd

Stools in the sleet

Wind torn cliffs

Dangle as

Washing line horizons rip.

And we're left;

A sloshing rinse bucket

In the machair,

Wondering if we'll ever see again

Our dear Éireann

Ireland walks down the isle of oceans, lifting her veil as she turns to us for a final look. For the last time I wave, and she is gone. The men stare out to sea, remembering the way of life they've left behind. As I wrap a shawl around Ma, she lifts her bony shoulders. Séan says her preparations are almost complete. He thinks she is turning into a bird, her fragile bones growing thin and light. Her slow, irregular heart soon to be a lapwing beat.

"Thank you, Mary-Anne, go now and look after your brother."

Weeks go by. Onboard, Hunger disguises itself and creeps around in a whisper. We have tried to drown it more than once, but it emerges, cold, blue and dripping from the shadows.

"Am I going to die?" Séan asks me worriedly.

The familiar shadow creeps into my head like coal scuttering into a bucket.

"No, of course not. You've just got a touch of fever, same as everyone here," I assure him.

The lower decks are crammed with people, but they are quiet. Some could almost be sleeping, but they're too pale and still. Hunger comes over to us occasionally, smoking a clay pipe.

Clinking glasses

And last redness of wine,

Hunger is drinking, rasping

Drunkenly

We fly, like tired birds. Along the line

Of forests, streams;

In our last sentence rhyme

Famine's gun is loaded, the crack

Sounding across

Mist, grass and bracken scents.

We pause on branches, commas

To admire the view

As a final full stop rends

The air.

Little Séan died in the night.

I cradled his poor weak body and stroked his hair as it happened, it was wispy and fine like duck fluff. Hunger blew smoke away from the gun barrel, and nodded to me, believing it was kinder to end his suffering. That night I refused to leave Séan's side, in my dreams I visited him, just as I had done with Father. We played together for a while, crunching sweet peas in the moonlight.

I dreamt that it turned to day and all the long sunlight hours yawned over purple moor grass. That our old smiles were back as we floated stick boats in the puddles, just like we used to. And that when the shadow of Hunger beckoned us one final time, we ran towards it, unburdened by dragging flesh. Like an old friend, he held our hands and together we walked, never breaking step. We waved to the orchid, bog myrtle and clover. We saluted the sinking bog land and castle ruin. And our hands shimmered to the strawberry roan who stood, forlorn, in the hazy Irish rain.

On the boat deck two dead children lay.

Their Ma stood still, indifferent or wise to the reality.

DUST ON THE ROAD
Joseph Burton
Folkestone, Kent

Winner of the Young Walter Scott Prize
16 to 19 age-group

The road to Vicksburg is a long one, but not without its scenery. Travellers are greeted by sweeping forests surrounding either side of the road in a great wooded embrace. In an automobile, this effect was enhanced; with the sky and the woods merging together in sweeping greens and blues.

So, as you can imagine, I was rather annoyed at having to stop.

But a gentleman has his duties.

Disembarking from the motor car, I straightened my clothes in a futile attempt to lessen the scorching afternoon heat. Finding myself in a glade – buzzing with life's activity in a great orchestral drone – I made my way over to the woman with roughly cut hair crouching by the side of the road who seemed to be oblivious of the heat despite her heavy clothing. The reason for my stopping.

She saw me before I could introduce myself; looking me up and down furtively like a forest animal. I cleared my throat regardless and began politely enough. "Are you lost?"

The woman took a moment before answering in a surprisingly well-spoken voice.

"You're not from around here."

I nodded as politely as could be expected. Something about this action made the crouching figure break into a smile. "From the north, I bet," she elaborated as if I was not standing before her.

Glancing around, off-put by the strange woman, I continued my endeavour. "I saw you while driving past: alone by the side of the road. Do you need a lift to the town? Or at least some water?"

The stranger shook her head for a moment, before seeming to think better of it. "I'll have some of that water," she stated, coming to a decision, before continuing to mutter under her breath almost with contempt, just loud enough for me to hear. "He's the optimistic sort I bet..."

Ready to defend myself, if not sure why, I rebuked her. "What did you say?"

"You think that the Depression will end in a year and there won't be another World War."

Her reply stopped me. I'd never really been affected by the Depression and the War was before my time. Besides, surely one was enough? Another would be simply ridiculous. Yet, something about her words triggered a rising anger within me.

"What do you know about war?" I demanded.

At this, the woman finally stood up to face me. "It will make me a living," she explained, as if I were doing something very amusing, "this place – all around you – it was a battlefield."

Despite myself I looked around at the glade. Her words somehow made the flourishing wildlife seem more sinister; parasitical. Nevertheless, I objected, not liking her mocking tone. "But the battle took place in the town."

Shaking her head, suddenly irritable, my strange acquaintance elaborated on her claim. "The Siege of Vicksburg in 1863 was only the centre of the conflict, various other undocumented skirmishes happened in places like these."

She spoke as if reading from a book. The factual detail of this astounded me and for some reason I had no doubt that she spoke the truth. "You seem to know your stuff," I commented, impressed.

A sudden hooting from the woods briefly caught my attention as the woman dismissed my surprise with her reply. "I studied the Civil War before the Depression hit. There were a lot of battles."

That final sentence seemed to sum up the American Civil War quite nicely. Personally, I had always held a certain fascination for the varied battle tactics and daring manoeuvres which history boasted. "Was it a good skirmish?" I asked innocently enough. "Was it a tale of heroic bravery and suchlike?"

The woman gave me a long, long look, to the extent that I became nervous, before eventually gesturing for me to follow her. I did as instructed, trailing behind my newfound companion as we trekked into the swampish glade. After a short while, the woman stopped and, taking a small shovel from a pocket in her coat, unearthed some of the wet reed-infested ground. She did so in a regular rhythm, for several minutes, parting the earth floor with its sky-facing layer, until she found her prize: a faded yet still shining golden ring. I stood transfixed throughout the entire ritual. The patient archaeologist handed me the item as if it was nothing of value.

"A man went to war with this, a promise of what was waiting for him at home."

I studied the ring as she spoke. Indeed, the afternoon light glinted off a name engraved into the polished metal, stating only: Anne. Before I could stop myself, a shiver flew up my spine, as if I was looking into a mirror and seeing death in my place.

Pleased by my reaction, my acquaintance continued, "And yet now, his faith is not even a footnote in history. We do not remember him. We do not know his name. But, nevertheless, he was as real as you or I. Such is the fate of us all."

There was a pause in which I was lost for words. Around us the forest life continued as ever, oblivious and uncaring towards my conflicted thoughts.

"Well, that was depressing," I said, suddenly wanting to break the silence, "do you still want that water?"

Seeming slightly disappointed, the woman nodded and we began to make our way back to the automobile, where I pulled out a bottle from under the driver's seat. I gave it to her with a hand that I could not stop from subtly shaking. Noticing this, the woman grinned softly before proceeding to gulp down the water. Obviously, she had not realised her own thirst. Again, not wanting to be allowed to think too deeply, I filled the silence.

"It's good to see that you're productively working your way back up to prosperity, in any case – "

"I'm looting a war grave," she interrupted briefly, pausing from her drink, "but, yes, go on."

I repressed my opinions on that matter admirably before continuing, "My friends in town will never believe what happened here..."

"Friends?" The woman spoke up again, as if it was an almost unbelievable fact.

"Yes, I'm going to meet them in Vicksburg, for a book club."

Again, there was a long silence.

Again, I filled it, gesturing to the car beside us. "In my trusty Model T, 1924 motorcar."

The pride in my voice was uncontainable. At the time, I really did cherish that vehicle. The first one I ever had.

"Of course, now it would only sell for a hundred dollars or so..." I concluded reluctantly.

Something I said caused the face of my acquaintance to light up, as if suddenly struck by a thought. A surge of pride went through me that my cherished transport could cause such a reaction. I elaborated smugly, "It's been a real friend to me on this journey of mine; travelling around the southern states, visiting friends and family. Taken me all the way from Chicago."

Nodding slowly, still in thought, the woman replied, "I was saving up for a car like that before the Depression. Learnt to drive and everything."

Suddenly turning to me, my new companion spoke again. "Look, you've been kind to me, giving me this water, so how about you help yourself to something from what I found today."

I frowned, "You mean I can take whatever I want from your war loot?"

She nodded. For a moment my historical fascination conflicted with my respect for the dead. Seeing my indecision, the woman prompted me, "From dust they were made and to dust they have returned. What do a few trinkets matter to them now?"

Despite my earlier repulsion at the thought, I am sad to record that I agreed with her eagerly. Smiling, the woman pointed me towards where I had first seen her by the road. I now noticed that a bag – like its owner, worn at the straps – lay there, with the sparkle of hidden treasure inside.

I ran over to it like a child towards a present.

Crouching down as my acquaintance had done not so long ago, I opened the sack to reveal the articles within; buckles from uniforms, loose currency and the occasional rusted weapon glared back at me, as if from the tomb of a forgotten age.

However, before I could reach inside I noticed that I still had that simple, golden ring in my hand. The lover's name sat, set in the metal, as dead as ever.

"To dust they have returned," I remembered the woman saying. Leaving only food for the now sickening plants and these items of tarnished metal.

As I thought this, I felt a breeze cross my face and the spurting sound of an engine starting. I turned just in time to see my automobile, that cherished transport, being driven away by the woman who had found a better way to make some money and survive. She was gone before I could even shout, her passage pushing the dust from the road into my face and making me sag to my knees in a coughing fit. Neatly reversing our original positions.

The sun struck down on me. The glade buzzed. I lay on the damp ground for a few minutes, trying to catch my breath and my fortitude. Still by my side, the bag full of the dead's property was my only companion. I realised that I would need to start making my way to the town at some point, but somehow I could not bring myself to move. It was as if I was as lifeless as the dust blowing over me like the ashes of time.

So, there I lay, amongst the dead. On the long road to Vicksburg.

TRANSMIGRATION PROGRAMME
Helena Baxendale
Bradford on Avon, Wiltshire

Shortlisted

Jakarta, Java, Dutch East Indies 1942

As the rest of the world rages its war against itself, and Indonesia falls occupied by Japanese forces, forever eating its tail in a tangled mess of destruction and fear, in some strange and confusing sense our lives lie blissfully untouched by the perils that our brothers face in far off lands of war and, although radio and telegraph allow for threat and fear to ripple down the wires and into our lives, we are safe. Crowded, threatened maybe, but untouched still.

A boy winds through a web of networking alleys, colours, cycles, carts and sirens. A cable forest interlaces the crooked houses and streets into being. Oily fumes and lively spices infuse the moving air with Jakarta itself. People - people perched nursing babies in doorways, people shouting, people driving cattle, a rich man in his shiny, ebony-black, Chrysler automobile, purring through the busy streets. Jakarta's people, the people that live and breathe the lively region. A persistent perfume of coal, spice and earth wriggles into every sigh, every shout, every note sung from an open window, every breath. The city breathes... Jakarta, a structured and complex ecosystem of beings. Loving and living and breathing.

This is Arif.

A girl wanders through the thick green of the forest. This is her terrain, the place she knows and the place her spirit thrives. She works her way between the intricately woven vines, her limbs tensing and flexing to dance through the jungle with skill and accuracy, to the place she knows, to the place, the small glade, where it began. Her trees.

"When a baby is born, three trees must be planted, one for the placenta, one for the name, one for the baby, they can never be cut down or hurt."

And sapling and child should live and thrive together leaf to heart, to blood and soul as they grow ancient and wise.

This is Lia.

Arif

Envelopes containing fire-igniting letters, written in incomprehensible code, were strewn across tables in despair. Transmigration Program, Colonisation, Sumatra: words resounded above my head, adult conversations in desperate, hushed voices. Our community, our buzzing corner of Jakarta sliced open by fear and unknowns. Our community, my family, was washed with a flood of worry and unfinished answers. Our home was slipping through our fingers, and there was nothing we could do.

Lia

I have never met a soul outside our small tribe, the Orang Rimba, I am one of merely 3000 individuals in our race. Here we have lived, in Sumatran rainforests since the dawn of time, undisturbed and at one.

Arif

I didn't understand, I couldn't understand, but sure enough there was a fleet of huge, curvy glistening buses, lined up in a row, with drivers and mechanics in front cranking the oily handle to shuttle us to the edge of nowhere. To the vast ocean. There I was, alongside countless others on the colourless road into the future.

Surges of people engulfed me in a tide of bodies as we were crushed onto the heaving steamer, belching black smoke. Jakarta had imprinted itself deeply in my heart. The churning water stabbed agony within my soul. But my pain didn't matter, not to the authorities.

Lia

Visiting my birth trees. That once were. That once lived alongside me. That were gone.

One stump. Pain.

Two stumps. Nameless.

Three stumps. Obliterated and inexistent. Murdered.

Hot tears rushed to my eyes and cold fear stirred in the pit of my stomach.

I tore through the forest. Tears streaming down my face in rivulets and mingling with the mud at my feet.

Arif

I had watched as the land became fainter and thoughts became memories, more and more inky water between my home and me.

I would never return. My last look at Java, and an unforgotten life.

Lia

"Lia, something's wrong!" My mother screamed, the sound slicing through the listening trees.

I ran to her, pressing my face into her chest, my breath catching dryly in my throat and tears staining the cloth of her cloak. Crying and crying, to her, the sky and the forest that caved in around us to feel our aching hearts.

Arif

We had been in awkward, half settlement stages for over a month. Dead houses and anaemic streets obliterated any fleeting spirit in where we lived. The water ran tired from an unknown source - but I knew the authorities weren't mustering water from thin air. They revelled in their power but even they couldn't control the elements. Fumes rose up from factory crop processes that ate away at the land the more that we ate away at them. Father struggled away in the plantations, mother sat wilted and alone in the dark, hot interior of our regulation house. A marching divide breathed down our necks asking our conscience questions we didn't want to answer. Our pallid ring of nothing, crept forward like a blood stain, eating away at the dense green. Swathes of vines were swept back desperately like fraying ribbons of emerald cloth, rich jade, shrinking back from concrete grey.

It was those unanswerable questions revolving in my mind that set me to break the rules.

Lia

New, dead-leafed plants that produced a bitter fruit that burned on the tongue and made the head spin, began to replace the natural forest that we knew, and the birth trees of our ancestors and relatives were purged from us like a terrible plague, filling us with a hard, black, fiery agony that ripped and tore at our hearts from within. An empty battlefield fell over the land, where stood the slashed stumps of the birth trees. Our trees. The trees of the earth. And our beginning.

Our home fallen in ruin and despair, a starved, hurt congregation gathered from the last embers of life in our peoples. After vague discussion an expedition was soon planned; we would stop the exterminating force that destroyed and killed like nothing else.

Watching as the men loaded up reed caskets, I smiled in surprise upon seeing my father striding towards me with my own woven pack. He handed it to me, heavy, but I was strong. This time I would not stay home with the women and children.

We journeyed without rest, moon and sun casting iridescent shadows, dark and light merging jade and gold. Suddenly figures became shadows, vines, leaves. Clammy realization hit me in the face.

I was alone. Lost to the will of the rainforest.

Arif

I stole out of the house, knife in hand. Gripping it in my hot palm as I edged between the bars that forbade and held the forest beyond… Searching for truth, reality, life. I thought I was alone, I was wrong.

Lia

He had coffee-dark hair and an olive complexion; a knife clasped in his hand. In his eyes was bitter displacement alongside glimmering determination and brilliant sparks of adventure.

Arif

Her striking, all-seeing green eyes peeked from beneath her tousled hair with intense curiosity and beauty; she stood perfectly, embedded in her own environment. Her strong sinewy limbs moved her through the trees like a monkey or a tigress, agile on her feet.

No longer alone.

Scintillations of new lightness shimmered through their veins electrically. Walking to the end of the forest, together.

Answers to questions didn't matter; truth, life, the future, did.

One girl - a child born of the forest,

One boy - displaced yet not lost,

were going to change Sumatra, Indonesia, the world. Because they cared. For the earth and the people and lives that mattered within it. And they would not let it die. They made a difference. Two young people changed minds and lives, histories and futures forever. But there was more to be done.

Lia and Arif lay beside the river as elderly man and woman, tuned in perfectly to the gentle, contented swish and pulse of the water, as a leaf, tender-green, fresh and untouched, allowed itself to be carried silently across the moving water. Hope.

Lestari,

Lestari, Everlasting. That is what my name means in our language. This story is our story, it is of my dear ancestors who live on in my heart, and the retelling of it voiced by my mother and my grandfather when I was a small child. I feel it to be my duty to sustain my ancestors' lives for as long as I live. The change they made and the life they lived together always inspires me, and of course as I sit here now in the dappled shade beside the water, I recite it to my own children as they rest, peacefully in my lap. Everlasting. And we are safe.

ALIEN BOUNCERS
Frankie Browne
London

Shortlisted

"For the last time, we are not watching *Hello, Dolly!* again!"

Mum has said this not for the first time today. I go outside before the wrath of my six-year-old brother Mark is unleashed on her, Kevin the gardener and my well-being. Honestly, my well-being is virtually non-existent today anyway, but it's a keen hobby of Mark's to make sure that it never shows its face.

"I want to watch *Hello, Dolly!* right now!" is repeated again and again from a voice-box turned up to full volume (I've been to Dr. Hills twice, thinking I've become deaf at the hands of Mark). The peaceful streets now echo my brother's desires. I grab a beach ball from our front yard and gently bounce it along as I run down our road, trying to pretend I have no relation to the cries. I'm good at it when Dad's around.

I continue to bounce the ball as I take in what a beautiful day it is. It's really swell: the grass is green, the smell of flowers fill my nose, the sky is blue and the sun is making a centre-stage appearance. I wonder if today's significance is affecting the weather.

Is it a coincidence?

Yes.

I continue to bounce the ball, over and over, but I don't know why.

Am I trying to occupy my mind?

Maybe.

I think for a bit.

Probably.

I think some more.

Definitely.

Of course I'm trying to occupy my mind! Why am I even asking myself that? I stop bouncing the ball and kick it as hard as I can in anger. The ball rockets away, making a crash landing plop into a neighbour's pond.

I give up and trudge home, looking down at the soft green grass. It comforts me a bit as I reach our yard. Mark's wrath has been silenced for now. But I hear the annoying buzz of excitement as it begins to rouse in the sitting rooms of our neighbourhood. It's a buzz which I'm sick of. I slam our front door and stand still in the hall. Silence. Until I hear the TV being turned on.

"Eric!" Mum calls from the sitting room.

I kick off my shoes and quietly walk towards the fuzz of CBS. I stop before coming in, I have a moment of feeling cold. I mean really cold. I shiver and ready myself to cry. But Mum already has me wrapped up in her warm arms as she rocks me to and fro. We weep for a few minutes but then Mum kisses me on the head and we both feel a bit better.

"I know it's hard but you need to watch this," whispers Mum. "It's important to us, it's important to everyone. And probably really important to Dad."

I quietly giggle. "I hope it's important to Dad."

Mum properly laughs at this. "Me too!" she says.

We hug for a while until Mum gradually lets me go.

She looks at me. "Shall we go in?" she asks.

I nod my head and we go in together, holding hands. My newly found positivity takes a considerable dive as I see Mark, slouching on the sofa with a bin on his head. He clutches a piece of paper which displays the barely legible phrase: 'I WANT TO WATCH HELO DOLY'. It is written in red.

"Take that off," demands Mum.

"Never," says Mark, his voice's volume doubled under the bin.

"If you don't take that bin off your head, I will do bad things to you, Mark Armstrong!" fumes Mum.

"If you threaten me, Janet I will unleash - "

Before Mark can unleash whatever destruction he thinks he can cause, the cure for his anger is aired on TV in the form of Walter Cronkite. Mark immediately takes the bin off his head and beams in wonder at the anchorman. For some reason, Mark loves Walter Cronkite. He is his biggest fan. One night, I woke up in terror when I heard Mark constantly quote Walter Cronkite from next door. 'And that's the way it is' was the one which woke me up sweating. Mum and Dad have no idea why my little brother is such a fan but they don't care. As long as it shuts Mark up, it's all hunky dory.

I hope it will remain hunky dory as the broadcast begins. Much to the dismay of Mark, Walter Cronkite is replaced with a circle. The circle has many tones and variations but it's certainly not Earth. It's the moon and a dotty line is drawn round it a few times until it suddenly droops directly on to the fuzzy sphere. Just above the droop, some edgy words appear: *Lunar Module* it reads.

Then it's gone. And something I've never seen before fades onto our screen. I can't tell if it's real or not but it looks like a silver tin, covered in golden wrapping paper with three straws sticking out of it. That's enough for Mark to cry out, place the bin over his head and retreat. The escape is in vain as Mark unknowingly runs into the door. Mum quickly rushes over and places him on her lap before he has any idea what's hit him. I did find it funny but not funny enough to stop myself looking at the so-called CBS simulation.

Below the tin rocket is grey cheese. It's going on for miles and miles. Is it really cheese? I think about it for a few moments until I decide not to discover the deadly truth. The truth I still haven't truly realised is that Dad's in the rocket tin.

I look at Mum. "Is Dad in there?"

She glances down at me. "Well I hope so."

I stare back at the TV.

The moon is the closest land to Earth and it's been here for all existence. It's a place which the world relies on and yet no one from our world has been to it. It just happens to be my dad paying a visit for the first time. I see the moon almost every night, shining like a mirror ball, the mirror ball of the universe, partying away. If Dad succeeds, he's going there to dance. If he fails, he's going there to be thrown out by some alien bouncers or something. This is the best symbolism I can make up.

The screen now depicts something even stranger: the same tin rocket my dad's in now flying in the midst of a black landscape, with fire blasting from the base. It's still some weird simulation but nonetheless damn incredible.

Walter Cronkite has lost his power in Mark's mind, the spaceship is now in charge. Mum is simply watching, I don't know what she's thinking but she's thinking a lot. Her eyes are full of thought.

The screen changes once more. We see from the ship's perspective as the moon looks more cheesy than mind can explain. The rocket is gradually moving across the craters until it stops.

Silence as the TV crackles with Cronkite's voice, intertwined with Dad's, Buzz Aldrin's and Mike Collins'. The simulation shows the tin rocket slowly lower. Then very simply, it lands.

THE LUNAR MODULE HAS LANDED, the TV reads.

And suddenly I hear from miles and miles away, from another world entirely, my dad say, "The Eagle has landed." My dad said that and it's not embarrassing, distressing or scary. But just very strange.

We no longer see the moon simulation but according to Mark, the next best thing: Walter Cronkite beaming away, rubbing his hands and exclaiming, "Whew Boy!"

A few moments later, broadcasting ends. I don't know what I do for the next six hours. Nothing I guess. I try to sit, I try to read, I try to sleep, I try annoying Mark (and succeed) but that's it. I find myself eventually sitting exactly where I was six hours ago, now wearing PJs, no longer seeing a simulation but instead the real thing.

It's much more fuzzy and the moon looks certainly less cheesy but that doesn't matter, because we're seeing the moon. The real moon and Dad is about to step on it. He looks different, partly because he's wearing a helmet but he doesn't look like Dad. He is Dad for only two people, a husband for one person and Neil Armstrong for the rest of the world. It seems like today he is only Neil Armstrong.

"I'm going to step off the ladder now," Neil Armstrong says.

He does.

Pause.

"One small step for man. One giant leap for mankind."

After that, I know life will be different for Mark and me. And as Mum walks outside to sudden crowds of reporters, I realise life will be different for everyone.

But my life has become strange.

I have neither been to the moon nor stayed on Earth.

I think I'm one who gets kicked out by the alien bouncers.

LITTLE MATRON
Catherine Fitzhugh
Stewarton, East Ayrshire

Runner-up

Moscow – 14 September 1812

There was a small fire in the street as our carriage rolled out the gates. Flames licked at a wall, beautiful in the way they flickered and danced, but the incident was not unusual – with the buildings being made of wood, it was often I could peer out the window and watch a man stamp fire out with his shoe. Today, however, there was no shoe, for my family and the horses that dragged us along were the only ones there. We were fortunate to live near the edges of the city, and so could afford to be amongst the last to leave. It had been two days since word reached us that Napoleon was to come to Moscow, and it seemed every living soul had left the city.

I sat nearest the window and looked out at the empty street, with Sofya curled up beside me. She had a silk headscarf draped over her, the design red and blue flowers, but curls of ebony hair had wriggled free and hovered over her eyes. She focused on those little ringlets with a grimace.

"Sonya," Ma said, "don't make that face. Children who frown grow more wrinkles." Our maid, Yelena, who was seated next to my mother, jolted at Ma's tone.

My sister's face smoothed, though there remained an agitated sparkle in her eyes. She had never liked our mother's pet name for her; she was very proud of the name she had been baptised under, Sofya. It made sense; my mother, though always well-meaning, had never hidden her thoughts – how plain her poor little Sonya was, how ashen and drab, so instead my sister clung to the part of her that she saw as pretty: her own name. Pretty little Sofya. I had the privilege as a boy to never hear what people thought of my outward looks. It was silly, I thought, to criticise the looks of a girl barely nine years old, but Ma said that was because I was the brother and brothers never thought about those things.

My sister shifted in her seat, her hands in her bag. She was looking for something, that much was clear, but in moments her search became erratic.

I put my hand on her shoulder, "Sofya, what's wrong? Hmm?"

"She isn't in my bag! There's Anastasya and Natalia, but Matryona isn't here! I think she fell out. Yes, she must have fallen out the bag as we were leaving, I did swing it a little." There was a pause, and then she removed two porcelain dolls from her bag, one with yellow hair in braids and the other with black hair and brown flecks of paint for freckles.

Ma's eyes darkened, "Sonya, we're not turning back for some toy! Besides, it will have broken if it hit the steps. There wouldn't be time to pick up the pieces, and it's no good with a hole in its face."

Sofya made a small sound, and sniffed. The thing with my sister was that she was good at making herself cry, she could do it at any time to get what she wanted, but her eyes changed colour – a pretty blue – when she was genuinely sad and there they were, a moment ago grey as steel and now sapphire gems.

I hid a sigh under a false cough. "But we are barely down the road." I hit the roof of the cab, and my father stopped the horses. Reaching for the door, I turned to Ma, "I'll go fetch it; I can walk fast." My eyes then met my sister's. "You say she must have fallen somewhere near the door?"

"Yes! If she is broken, you need to get every single piece! I'll have to glue her together."

When I stepped out, my father turned in his seat, "Where are you going?"

"I've forgotten something," I said.

"What is it? I'll go back–"

I shook my head, "No, I will go. I can run faster than you; I won't be a moment."

There was a look on my father's face; he opened his mouth to speak, and then shut it again. A man in a ragged coat ran past, and there was a gunshot in the distance. My father called out to the man, and they spoke at the front of the carriage in hushed tones, then my father looked at me, "The French are in the city; there's fire in Kitay-gorod. If you're going back, you'll need to be fast. Three minutes, you hear? Not back by then and we'll go without you."

The peasant man hurried away, and I turned on my heels towards the house. Our home, by no means the largest of houses but nonetheless comfortable, was at the top of a long road, while our carriage was now at the bottom. After I passed three houses, I started to run.

There was no doll, or pieces of doll, on the steps. I opened the door, which had been left unlocked. It was not in the front hall. Up the stairs, I went to her room and saw it on the floor beside her vanity. I suspected that Sofya had been playing with her dolls until the last possible moment; Matryona had been dropped much sooner than my sister thought. A pretty thing, too; I recalled when my mother had taken me to have it custom-made for Sofya's birthday. The doll's brown tresses were made from goat hair, the tinkerer had said. She wore a cerulean dress to match the lifeless painted eyes, but the garment we brought her home in was pale yellow. Sofya never kept the dolls' original clothes; she made dresses herself out of stockings and scarves, sewing buttons and beads onto her tiny creations.

I took a moment to look about the room, unsure when I would next see it; my mind stilled by the steady ticking of a clock. Tick tock, tick tock.

My heart leapt to my throat when outside there was a crash, and I ran to the window to see glass and broken wood sprawled out over the road. The French officers had arrived; they prowled over the cobbles, hounds slavering on the hunt for a fox. The door from across the street burst open, the door left attached on a single hinge, and a man appeared – no uniform, a Russian – and he leapt at a Frenchman. The fox had turned on the hounds, fangs bared.

A shout, then an explosion. Or I thought it was an explosion, though at first I saw nothing. The Russian had stopped his assault, statuesque before his rivals, when he collapsed face first against the floor. On his back, between the shoulder blades, a puddle of red expanded over his shirt.

My breath curdled in my throat; a noise ripped up from my chest. It was a howl more than a scream. Hot tears clogged my eyes, the world messy watercolours. My feet were numb, my fingers too, but I glanced down and saw my knuckles were a string of pearls for my grip on the doll.

An officer looked up at the window, he marched towards the door.

The back way was my obvious escape route. Down the corridor, through the little grey door, the spiral staircase the maid used. A draughty door with a bronze handle, it led to the patch of land with the chicken coop. I stepped right in the mud, so I hid the doll up my sleeve so my hands were free to catch my fall. As predicted, I tripped and when I reached the gate my legs were coated in wet earth from the knee down.

Out into the street behind the house, I saw that Hell had spat into Moscow. A fire had started in one of the houses, the flames lapped the wood and lurched into the windows of the house next to it, then the house next to that. It was not an immediate danger, the flames kept somewhat at bay by the autumn chill, though my stomach turned as I reminded myself there was nobody to put it out.

I headed to the bottom of the road and around the block to the street where I had started and peered around the corner at the street from behind a wall. The French were further ahead, too occupied with seizing the contents of stolen boxes to notice a little Russian boy at the end of the street turn pale because his family's carriage had disappeared.

There were shouts nearby, the whinny of horses – the last Russians leaving the city; the noise caused by increased panic. The idea arose that my father's carriage was still in the city, amongst the people, and my legs, shaky as they were, flew over the ground. I faltered around a corner when three men, stood before a house, appeared in my view. They were in conversation but their voices were indistinct; I saw one held a musket. My instinct was to run when one man shouted and his voice became clearer; he wasn't French.

The man that spoke turned then and saw me. His voice, thick and hoarse, echoed, "You don't wear a uniform. You're Russian, boy?"

"Yes, sir."

There was a pause as his dark eyes examined my face. "Where's your family?" I recounted my search for Sofya's doll and how my father must have relented when the French arrived. He nodded and then clapped his large hand against my shoulder, "The border is just a few minutes from here. We're waiting on a friend, then we're following Kutuzov's men to Ryazan – the French won't follow us there. That's where the last of us are headed."

I nodded but stayed silent. A moment later, a man appeared and we started toward the crowds.

The doll had been in my hand so long the porcelain was warm to touch. When I looked at it – the red circles on its cheeks, the pink dot of paint for the lips; the tiny necklace made from string – a tear welled in my eye.

Whenever Sofya received a new doll, she held a baptism where the doll would receive its name. Sofya always said names have meaning – she had found a book on the subject and absorbed its contents religiously, her newfound knowledge put to use on her dolls until the day she could apply it to real children. She had named this one Matryona, made from matryoshka, "little matron", for she was to be the leader of the dolls. When Sofya played with them, Matryona was the nurse; she looked after the others. Their names were important, too, though some meanings were more obvious than others. Natalia was 'birth of Christ', for she had been the favourite Christmas gift one year. Anastasya was 'resurrection', for she had been purchased to replace a beloved doll that had been irreversibly broken. Matryona was the protector.

I didn't know this at first. It was only when she first shared the name with me that I had asked why she chose it.

"Some of the others can be rather silly, she likes to keep them safe," Sofya said. "She protects me too, sometimes."

"Protects you from what?"

She shrugged. "If she's in my pocket, I don't trip as much, and if she's on my lap while at dinner then I won't burn my tongue. It's because that is what she likes to do, look after people. Anyone and everyone."

There were carriages further ahead, but we could barely move for the sea of bodies and I decided to stay with my new companions until we reached the road outside Moscow, where there would be a clearer path down which to run to them. The chill of the evening set in, and I held Matryona to my chest in silent prayer.

LEST WE FORGET
Megan Lintern
Chapmanslade, Wiltshire

Shortlisted

He is a bundle.

His flushed skin is fragile and fresh as morning dew, swaddled in cocoons of white linen. Wailing with petal-soft lips scrunched up, he fractures the stillness of the night with a brazen announcement: he has arrived. Strange calloused hands tremble as they grasp for his blanket: they brush across the brand-new body beneath, exulting at the life that flourishes there. Five fingers squeeze around one as the infant stirs, feeling the divots and the creases of the hand he holds. There is so much to touch, so much to learn. Around the child, shapes bustle blurrily, their edges hazed by the overwhelming light. Everything is so clean, so fresh, so pure – the air itself is new. The bundle is passed from one cradling arm to the next, each embrace more warming than the last. Around him, voices fill the air like perfume, tingeing his every breath with colour as soft hums of adoration erupt from a dozen smiling mouths. Everywhere, there is love. He has no need to cry.

He is an explorer.

On hands and knees, he crawls, overcoming every obstacle. Grass stains his pale knees green, but he scurries onwards with a dimpled grin. As he crawls, he coos to himself in a language that no one can yet understand with a wisdom that no one can yet comprehend. To him, each mole-hill appears a mountain, and in each bush a jungle; but he battles onwards with all the fearless bravado of a three-year-old child – until suddenly a shadow falls over his own. Squealing, he wriggles a little faster, but he cannot escape the hands that encircle him. He flies, scooped up into the sky, before plummeting back down into a pair of broad hands. Giggling, he accepts defeat and nestles into the arms as they carry him back to safety.

He is an aeroplane.

Two twig-legs poke from shorts he must still grow in to, and two grubby hands slice through the open air as he runs, faster, faster. The morning smells like bacon as he soars down the stairs with a 'nee-yumm', tripping over his flailing feet. Like a fledgling he hops about unsteadily, still uncoordinated in his ever-growing body. Behind him trails a smaller bird, a little boy waddling on stubby legs, always following but never quite catching up. He doesn't mind. Sunlight streams through the frosted window panes as they stumble down stairs, across the hall, and out the door. The whole world they find there is white. Snowdrifts pack around the bows of trees and entomb the once-green grass like spilt cream. Ice bites into the boys' skin as their fingers drag through it, pink against the white, compressing the crystals into balls. They pause a moment as their mother runs out to encompass them in woollen scarves, but then carry on their game. They build and build all morning – a snowman, a castle, a car – until blades of grass poke their heads through the diminished snow, and the boys collapse on the ground, satisfied.

He is a misfit.

Cradling the toad in his bare hands, he shushes his friends as they creep through the classroom. Five pairs of gleaming eyes flitter nervously about the room; five pairs of red-tipped ears listen restlessly for footsteps. They tiptoe faster, avoiding the squeakiest planks as they pick their way between desks and chairs towards the front of the room. A blackboard is mounted to the wall there, and airborne chalk glitters like fairy dust in a thick wedge of sunlight. The boy is too close now, he cannot wait any longer – darting forwards, he careens around the back of the teacher's desk to jerk open the top drawer. With a victorious smirk, he unfolds his fingers to place the fat toad upon the chalksticks that live there. It croaks throatily, gooey skin pulsating. It is a beast of a thing. Inflating its speckled throat, it nods to them brusquely as they stagger from the room, blood rushing with the thrill of the crime.

He is a lover.

Combing a hand through his mussed-up hair once again, he waits patiently on the doorstep, shoes shining spotlessly in the orange porch-light. A tie sits neatly around his neck, a waistcoat peeks from beneath his jacket, and brand-new cufflinks clinch his shirtsleeves. One heel thrums the doorstep softly as he waits, fidgeting nervously, until at last the door swings open and out she steps. She is light and laughter ringed by a mist of honey-hued perfume, her chestnut hair tumbling in chin length waves. Thin leaves of lace and silk drape over her shoulders and around her hips, shifting about her ankles with each breath of autumn breeze. The dress is the pink of clouds at dawn, and her smile shatters the night like the rising sun. Her hand is soft, the fingers delicate as they knit between his. Her chatter starts as a burble and swells to a stream as they make their way down the street – her voice is the music the stars above dance to. Somewhere in the distance, jazz music sings a tune of love. His heart hums along.

He is a man.

Just seventeen, but Conscription will have him. The recruitment officer watches through deadened eyes as he takes the pen in hand to scrawl out a signature. It is his duty to fight, his debt to Britain herself; and yet his heart sinks as he pours his name onto the page in black ink. Exhaling a shudder, he hands over the paper with his soul attached. In return, he is passed a khaki bundle – uniform. He will look dapper, he is assured by the officer. He does look dapper, he confirms that evening as he peers in the mirror… but his mother does not agree. As she enters the room, something inside her blanches, and her whole body is flung against the back wall. There, she trembles with sobs until his father leads her away with a solemn nod. They never mention the uniform again in that house, until the day he goes to war.

He is a soldier.

His dapper uniform is less so now that it is pasted thick with mud and grime. He clings to a gun with shaking hands, his knuckles white with cold and fear. Screams, gunshots, and bomb blasts chant a discordant din, surrounding him with an orchestra of death. Bullets sing rat-tat-tat like tinny laughter. They compose a staccato melody, pinging off metal with shrieking high-notes and thudding into dirt (or something softer) with a grim percussive beat. He hears his own heartbeat too, a Morse code SOS thumping against his throat. A scream fights its way to his lips, but he pushes it back down, holding his breath until the sound stops squirming inside him. They call this place the Somme, but he calls it hell. Crouched in a foot of water on the trench floor, he curses the place with all the spite he can muster as he bats at the fleas in his sleeves; but no amount of cursing can save him now. Slicing through the rain comes the knell of a whistle and that dreaded fatal order: "Over the top!"

He is a casualty.

Just another piece of cannon fodder, he is sprawled in a cement of blood and dirt. Agony rips through him in peals, wave after wave of soul-shredding pain that sears black spots into his vision. In a tortured howl, he calls out the only words that may save him yet: The Lord's Prayer. Kissing the air with each syllable, he begs for what will never be as he cradles the wound in his shoulder. The deep lesion leaches blood into the ground, where it blooms poppy-like across the soil. Each flower hovers a moment, glorious, then dissipates in the heavy rain. "Thy kingdom come…" The words come slower now. Each syllable trips across his tongue, tumbling out bewildered; a last-ditch plea for mercy. A lump sits in his throat, thick and heavy, throbbing with the things he never said. His thoughts drift to snow, to toads, and to a beautiful girl as the rain washes the tears from his cheeks with almost motherly tenderness. His heavy-lidded eyes close at last, and his ears stop hearing the sounds of war. Instead he hears the sounds of jazz, and he drifts there in his dreams.

He is a gravestone.

Deep in the mud of a forgotten French field, the Earth claims him for her own. In the meadow above, he stands proud; perfectly aligned with his brothers in arms – one more white cross etched with one more forgotten name. The headstones bloom with petals of marble, pure as life and cold as death. They are kept pristinely, yet they decay; while gratitude once swathed them in fine cloth, it now hangs in tatters about their outstretched arms. A legion of lives lies rotting in that field - it moulds alongside a promise, the bloodied oath of 'never again'. In the songless hush, the fallen chant a chorus of their own. It is not a tune we hear with our ears, but one we sense with our hearts. Their voices waver in the silence, but their message still survives; when we play the game of war, we pay the price in love and loss.

THE STATION
Natasha Mirus
Ringwood, Hampshire

Runner-up

The dark clouds of steam carried with it the freedom, which was only found far away from the city that had been her home both before and after the War. The station was normally empty when Lena fled to its comforting vacancy, the platforms deserted with only a few lights to keep her company, their warmth replacing the usual heat from the crowded city centre.

Her cream painted bench, sat against the wall at the very end of the wooden canopies over the tracks, was a cold and welcoming refuge of solace. A frequent visitor, Lena sat on numerous occasions for most of the night, simply watching the trains do what she never could. Leave. The familiarity of the repetitive churns of the wheels, and the harsh clicks of the slamming doors acted as a plea to follow, though she had never been able to. After the third week she'd stopped bringing her suitcase. Now she sat, a way of escape, just not physically.

The night was particularly fresh. A breath of mist floated across the platform, the frost had begun to creep back, a sneaky return after fleeing from the sun during the day. Lena hurried towards her usual position. She never minded the cold, the harsh sting of it helped to keep any memories of the War away from her tired mind. Her job in the shop was dull but Lena had refused to return to work as a nurse. The shop required little concentration. That was when she drifted away into the past, a place she no longer wanted to reflect on. Her visits to the station allowed her to contemplate the future; her goals, only small, as well as her dreams to travel, further away from the mud in France.

Lena's quickened steps suddenly stopped as she came within viewing distance of her bench. She would have company. Placed precariously on the edge of the wooden seat, a man sat, leaning forward with his arms crossed over his knees. Lena noticed the slight tremor in his hands, though it may have been from the November fog that was now heavily swirling around his feet. Hesitantly stepping forward, Lena thought he seemed familiar, though she had seen many faces of men, soldiers in the past four years. Everyone was a soldier now, she had given up searching for resemblances, faces in the street were just another thing she wanted to avoid. The man tensed back when she perched next to him, it was the only bench in the station and she admitted to herself that she wouldn't mind the presence of another.

Knowing the next train would arrive soon; she noted the absence of a case. Though Lena found it hard to believe someone else was comforted by the loud yet harmless sounds of the station, she knew there were many who came back from Europe worse than she had. She leaned her head against the wall, prepared to sit in the cold silence until one of them left. Lena was startled when a cough broke the emptiness of the night and his muttered apology at her obvious surprise caused a change in her plans. She turned to him with a warm smile, one frequently used to comfort those once under her care.

"Are you catching the next train out Sir?" Lena didn't want to pry too much, but her curiosity meant that this was temporarily overlooked.

He looked hesitant, a guarded expression she was all too familiar with. "I'm not- " Another cough. "I am, yes."

Lena remained silent, the quiet falling over them again, but she knew he would not remain like this for long.

"Poole, then hopefully out of England from there but I'll- " he paused.

Taking this as a cue to cut in Lena responded happily, "Is this an impulse trip?" she asked, pointedly noting the lack of luggage.

This drew a laugh from her companion. "A bit like that yes, I've been meaning to leave for a while. I've never been keen on the city."

Lena gave a hum of agreement. "It can be a bit much. I hope to travel someday, a similar plan to you I suppose, but I've always found an excuse not to." Looking down in embarrassment, worried she had over shared, she noted a white scar running from the back of his hand, disappearing under his sleeve.

"I've decided not to miss any opportunities, not since - " The man paused again. Lena noticed he did that a lot. Despite the abrupt end to his explanation they both knew what he meant. Not since the War.

A slow rumbling made its way to the station; the low turns of the wheels produced a clumsy melody, filling every corner of the shelter in which they sat. The welcoming smell of steam washed towards them. The familiarity of the train's whistle graced a smile upon her lips. Slowing to a halt in front of them, only one door clicked open. The man stood quickly, already leaning in the direction of the door. Lena remained seated, frowning when the returning sense of longing to board appeared. Nothing was stopping her, she rented a house with another nurse, with whom she barely talked; she had no family left in the city, no obligations.

Almost missing the friendly good bye the man had offered, Lena hurried after him quickly, not allowing herself to change her mind. Reaching the carriage door first, stumbling up the steps she let herself take a breath. The dark red interior and the contrasting warmth did nothing to settle the excitement that was bubbling in her chest, causing a grin to spread across her features as she turned to the man just making his way onto the train.

"Poole, was it?' she questioned, following his gesture to one of the many empty compartments.

"Poole," he agreed, amused. "Then anywhere after that, it's up to you now. Quite a change of heart there, Miss."

Lena laughed brightly. "I've decided not to miss any opportunities," she said, repeating his words, adding, "not since the War."

THE PIPER
Andrew Pettigrew
The Royal Blind School, Edinburgh

Shortlisted

Portsmouth, England, 11 December 1915

Pain.

So much pain.

It was a storm, whirling inside me, shredding my heart like a bairn carelessly yanking off a rose's petals — delicate, precarious, pathetic petals. Or was it an animal, its talons clawing at my heart, vicious, untamed?

Or was it merely memory ...?

I sat up in bed, gasping, precipitation oiling my skin. I stared down at the sheet of paper in my lap, the candlelight trickling over its perfect, perfect whiteness.

Don't look. Don't. Look.

But I did, timidly glancing to my left, catching sight of a fellow patient, lying as if dead on perfect, perfect whiteness; my eyes darted back to the page.

Write, I told myself. Write something — anything.

Hesitation, a pause, silence. Then — with the lead pencil quivering in my hand — I began to trace words onto that blank landscape.

***

Loos, France, 25 September 1915

'Right, boys.' The Lieutenant Colonel stood before us, his uniform immaculate, his eyes glinting like fresh ice. 'You know what we are going to do out here today. This is for Scotland. This is for Britain. Today, Gerry will wish he never saw a Scotsman in a kilt in his whole life!'

The lads around me cheered, their faces shining as if bathed in starlight. Alistair grinned at me — a true, boyish smile that illuminated his whole face. My smile in return was faint, tremulous, a slither of fear slipping down my spine.

The Colonel noticed. 'Scared, young Angus?' he sneered, a growl brushing his voice as he stepped towards me menacingly. 'Not still wishing you had that feather in your hat, eh, you coward?'

A silence fell, icy eyes glaring at me. And then a single word, chased with harsh laughter — Conchie.

Conchie.

I stared down at my boots, shame prickling inside me, but defiance too, hot and smarting. I glanced back up, words forming on my chapped lips, but the Colonel had already resumed.

He told us our objectives, the consequences of failure, the necessity for victory. Patriotic jargon, I thought mutinously, hefting my bagpipes. Pointless.

'So that is the procedure,' the Colonel concluded. 'Good luck, boys.' He glanced at me, smirking. 'Or girl, I should say.'

More laughter, more jeers. Alistair touched my shoulder, his expression warning me not to rise to the bait. Well, I reflected resentfully, what was a pacifist if he picked a fight?

'Over the top, then, boys!' the Colonel yelled, and off we ran, swarming over the top like rats scampering out of a gutter.

I faltered. Stared. Gaped, eyes widening in horror.

The landscape that unfurled before me was a sight upon Hell itself. Wreathed in dancing, serpentine coils of yellowish fog, the ground was blanketed with the dissected limbs of shattered trees, painted with cloying mud and scarred by deep, jagged craters that sent plumes of smoke high into the air. A hundred yards away, I saw what seemed to be vast, metallic weeds, strangled callously by the earlier thunderstorm of shells and fire that we had sent their way.

The sky spilled out above us, ragged and bleak as if dying, yet it was gilded with ornate silver as the sun slowly, tentatively, peered upon the massed bodies that moved forward beneath it.

'Angus, quicker,' Alistair murmured, giving me a gentle shove, urging me on. 'Stop thinking of yer poetry an' play them pipes!'

I was about to respond, already raising the chanter to my lips, when at that moment someone screamed. A choked, strangled scream, pierced through with horror and shock that clenched my heart like an iron fist. Sudden fear flowed through the ranks, spreading like the ripples after a stone hits the surface of a loch.

And then the realisation — gas! Whether it was the wind or the hand of fate, I didn't know or much care; all that mattered was that our gas had come back to kill us.

'Angus, come on!' Alistair shouted, voice desperate, eyes blazing as he tugged me along, as we all ran onwards.

Men fell with hoarse cries, their lungs burning, the mud sucking greedily at their uniforms as their hands clawed frantically at their chests.

But we did not stop, and, as the music swelled from my pipes — 'Blue Bonnets over the Border', the one we all knew and loved — I turned from the weak, idiotic pacifist loathed by all but Alistair, to the Piper. It was as if the music swept away the fear, the anxiety, the panic the gas had caused. We were Scots after all, and, even though the idea of killing other human beings repulsed me, Scots are Scots.

And so we went on, charging towards the enemy trenches, and more and more men crumpled as they inhaled the gas, as if Death himself had swatted them down; but still we ran ... until the Germans opened fire.

The lad in front of me, Jamie his name was — a raw Kitchie, like me, young and inexperienced — suddenly collapsed, blood blooming across his chest as a bullet bit into his heart. He was dead before he kissed the ground, another stolen Scottish soul.

* * *

The pencil skittered across the page as I lost focus for a moment, blinded, reeling. The smoke, the putrid stench of decay ... gunfire ...

Blood.

Even now it still ached, still hurt, still ripped.

Nearly there. We're nearly there noo, nearly made it. Come on.

'Are you all right, son?'

I started. The man to my left was not a corpse after all, but was sitting up, gazing at me with — kindness? Concern? Bemusement, even?

'I ... I'm fine,' I stuttered, realising then that I was crying. Oh, treacherous tears. Hastily, I wiped them away, but no doubt he'd noticed.

'If yer sure.' The man leant back against his pillows, unconvinced. He was a large man, now I came to look at him, with broad shoulders, rugged skin, and eyes the shape and colour of almonds. 'What you writing there?'

'Just ... memories,' I answered feebly. So much for being a poet! I thought ruefully.

'Memories? We've aw got those, son.' Those almond eyes seemed to peer out of caverns now, haunted and vulnerable. 'So many losses!' the man whispered, sorrow weighing his words. 'But we aw do the best we can, tae stop 'em. Didn't you, son?'

I nodded. But had I? Had I honestly done the best I could, to prevent those deaths? To prevent ... to stop ... his ...

I fought back my tears, holding them prisoners in my head this time, for what would this man, this veteran — as he seemed one — think of me, greeting like a wee lass?

I turned back to my paper, a fresh determination to continue, to get this all over with, seizing me.

'O'er by Christmas,' I heard the man mutter. 'That's what they told us. O'er by Christmas... what a bunch of codswallop that was.'

* * *

Chaos. All was chaos, the air torn apart by a constant snarl of gunfire, bullets tearing into men to my right and left, the wind forcing the scent of sweat and smoke and dirt into my nostrils —

And the blood. Oh God, the blood! It saturated the earth like glistening ink, soaking the bodies, the bayonets, even the folds of my kilt. A fog was gathering in my head, blotting out what I was really seeing, so in fact I could not tell Scotsman from German, friend from foe.

But was there a difference? Really?

I stumbled, bile licking my throat, and Alistair — my good, strong, brave brother — grasped my forearm, saving me from joining the others in the muck.

'Nearly there,' he promised, like he had when we were wee, fleeing our ma like terrified magpies. 'We're nearly there noo, nearly made it. Come on!'

And it was no lie, either. As my pipes sang, as my muscles screamed from the constant movement, Gerry's front line trench was just yards away. We were so close — so close.

And then — pain. So much pain. A shard of corroded metal had shot into the air, stabbing straight into my thigh, a piece of shrapnel as sharp as a dagger. I let out a yelp of surprise, before crashing into the ground.

'Angus!' Alistair was above me, his face pale and distraught. 'I can help — it's OK —'

'Go!' I interrupted, my words coming out as an agonised shriek. Go. Please. Go.

Was it cowardice that I felt relief, knowing I wouldn't have to maim another soul? No. It was also the knowledge that the longer he stood there, the more chance he would get shot.

'Go!' I reiterated, this time louder, screaming at him to leave, to go on. 'Go!'

And as he obeyed, I caught sight of my pipes lying on the ground in front of me. My leg protesting violently, I crawled towards them, gathering up the old things as if they were a bag of gold, precious and beautiful.

And so I played, there on the wet soil, singing the words in my head like a prayer.

Many a banner spread,

Flutters above your head,

Many a crest that is famous in story ...

The gunfire clattered, the harsh wind stung my face, muffling the howls and strangled cheers that mingled strangely as the battle raged on.

... Mount and make ready then,

Sons of the mountain glen,

Fight for the Queen and the old Scottish glory ...

Fight for the old Scottish glory. I looked up, suddenly, my eyes smouldering in the smoke, and that's how I saw it happen.

Alistair was just short of the ruined barbed wire, his rifle steady in his strong hands as he sprinted towards the enemy — towards the bullet that slammed squarely into his skull.

No.

No.

For a single heartbeat, my brother — another son of the mountain glen — stood, swaying slightly: a marble sculpture teetering on the edge. And then, another volley of bullets blasted him off his feet, tossing him aside like a marionette whose strings had been cut ...

'No!' The word ripped through my throat, a single, unbearable note of purest misery. 'Alistair!'

Please, I thought wildly, desperately trying to drag myself towards him. Please, don't be dead, don't be dead.

My heart thumping, breath rasping, I reached his side. I grasped his shoulders, imploring him to wake, touching his soot-encrusted face between my fingers, feeling his pulse ...

And found it silent.

A terrible silence in the midst of terrible noise.

Hot tears pricked my eyes, cascading down my cheeks like bitter rain as I stared into the vacant eyes of my brother, already gone, as the world spun around us like a cruel carousel of death and sorrow. Why wasn't I dead too?

Why hadn't a shell blasted me to scraps by now?

I wanted to die.

I wanted to be with my brother, not here, on a plain in a foreign country where Death roamed as a plague.

Oh, Alistair.

* * *

I paused, my pencil suspended over the page, waiting for fresh words that would not come.

Did I want to die? Would Alistair have wanted me to die?

'Blue Bonnets over the Border.'

I looked up. The man in the other bed was staring across at the paper in my lap, a slight, mournful smile playing across his lips.

'What?' I demanded, a spark of anger kindling within me — how dare he read over my shoulder? My own private words?

'Blue Bonnets over the Border,' he repeated, and he chuckled — actually chuckled. 'Lad, if you played that on yer pipes fer so long, ah'd thought you'd know it by now. March, march, Ettrick and Teviotdale! Why the deil dinna ye march forward in order?'

'March, march, Eskdale and Liddesdale,' I finished. 'All the Blue Bonnets are bound for the Border.'

He grinned at me. And for a moment, I was reminded of that smile. That true, boyish smile that seemed to illuminate his whole face. And in that smile, I found comfort. I found resolve.

And I found myself, once again — the Piper.

THE LONG SUNSET
Jonathan Rhys Clark
Chorlton, Manchester

Shortlisted

Author's note

The Long Sunset *is set in the early seventh century after the fall of Rheged. Rheged was a dark-age kingdom which is thought to have been roughly equivalent to modern Cumbria. Bernicia is now Northumbria while the fort of Catraeth is most likely modern day Catterick. Urien, Owain, Llywarch, Taliesin and Theodoric are all genuine historical figures. The battle in the story is based on the Old Welsh poem* The Battle of Argoed Llwyfain *by Taliesin. In fact, the exchange between Owain and the messenger of Theodoric, along with the speech of Urien and the quote "It was as easy as sleeping" all come, more or less directly from the poem.*

It had been raining all day, but now the spring breezes had blown the heavy clouds away over the eastern hills, and the setting sun's light was catching on the raindrops in the cattle pastures. I, Tudual, was making my way back to the settlement tired from a hard day's labour and hungry for bread and meat and a warm fire to dry myself beside. There were only a few of us there now. Back in my father's day, things had been different. There had been a prosperous settlement of both free and bondmen here under the authority of a chieftain. But plague had taken the people, and the chieftain had fled south. So now there was just a handful of us with no ruler and little protection from any foes. I sighed to myself as I approached the main gate and looked over my shoulder down the way I had come. Then I gave a start, for riding across the open field, his long shadow stretched out behind him, came a man sat on a pony clasping something to his side.

I gave a shout, "Hoi, traveller, are you seeking shelter?"

He kicked his horse's flank and cantered towards me.

"Aye, if you are offering?"

"Indeed, and if you are a bard, as your harp," for that is what he was carrying, "would suggest, then we would be delighted if you were to sup with us."

"I will sup with you."

We neared the gate and seeking to make conversation, I asked him what his name was. He didn't look up, but I saw the ghost of a smile dance around his mouth.

"I am the singer of songs and the teller of tales. That much shall I say."

"Who is your Lord then?"

At this his face darkened, "My Lord is dead. I can take no other."

He spoke no more and we entered through the gate of the settlement.

"Father!"

I looked up to see my second son, Brice, dashing towards me.

"Eanfled has gone into labour, early. Edryd is most distressed."

Edryd was my oldest son, being eighteen summers old and Eanfled the girl he had wed last summer. Her parents were Angles from Deira who had come west seeking land and had settled together with several of their kinsmen in our community. Now she was bearing my son's child, but her time had come sooner than expected. I rushed into my son's cottage.

"But Mother, I cannot leave her!" I heard Edryd say.

"You can and you must. This is women's work and you will only make matters worse." She looked up and saw me approaching. "Take him to the Great Hall and take his mind off things. He's rather shaken."

Brice went to see to the pony and I put my arm round Edryd's shoulders. "Come on son, it will alright. Why, I've told you many times of how it was when you were born."

I felt his breathing relax. "Right, Father."

We entered the Great Hall. In former days it had been the domain of our chieftain. He however had fled south with our king, Llywarch. Now it was empty with none feeling they could step up and claim it for their own. We mostly used it for work, and in the evenings the men would gather there to eat and to drink ale. I led Edryd and my guest towards the benches.

"Alright, Edryd?" asked Penwyn, my wife's brother, looking up from his drinking horn.

He nodded shakily, "Yes thanks."

"And who's this?" barked Carranog, the smith, gesturing at the bard by my side. "Sing can he?"

"Oh, I can sing. Oh yes."

"If you are a bard then you must serve a king," Brice began but the bard cut in.

"If you must know of my Lord then I will tell of him."

He stood in the middle of the hall with his eyes almost completely shut. I sat back against the animal pelts and listened to the crackling of the fire and the gentle spring breeze gliding above the thatch roof. And this is what I heard.

"My Lord was Urien son of Cynfarch, ruler of Rheged and his son Owain. I was his court bard. Greatest of all the princes of the North, was he, generous to all, valiant in battle and the protector of his people. He was the greatest since Arthur, greater in truth, since in Arthur's day the rot was only just creeping in. In my Lord's time it had struck far deeper than he realised. He had a dream, that the people of this Island could unite, that the heathen could be cast back into the sea from whence they came and that the light of this our land should never go out. Alas that it was not to be!

The greatest moment came one morning, nearly ten years ago now. Theodoric, king of Bernicia, known as Flamebearer, enemy of the Cymru, marched on Rheged. I was there in the fort of Catraeth when the message came. Theodoric had brought an army down the coast. Four hosts strong they were, we were outnumbered.

I remember well the hustle and bustle in the fort. Shields being slung over shoulders, horses being mounted, swords sharpened, prayers said, and not all to the Christ. Urien and Owain just stood there calmly on the ramparts watching on. And then we were ready, the host of Rheged, riding to death or victory. I rode with them singing boldly of Gwen Ystrat and of Bremenium and the military triumphs enjoyed there. But deep down inside I felt a sense of cold dread.

We rode down the old Roman road. Our scouts reported that they had encamped in Llywfain Wood, on the east side of the road. Urien therefore gave orders for his men to raise their standard on a hillock just west of the road. There it was, the Raven Banner, woven by the Queen Modron herself, fluttering courageously in the breeze. The men dismounted and drank from the water skins their shield bearers had brought. It was always the worst, that waiting for the enemy to appear, and I could tell by the way Urien paced back and forth, heedless of the bracken, that he felt the same.

At long last Theodoric's envoys approached with a handful of men. They were bearing branches as a sign of truce and one of them spoke in our tongue.

"Will you give hostages to us? If you do we shall return with our war host to Bernicia and we shall not harry your lands any more. If not, then we shall make an end of you and your people. Prepare your hostages for my Lord is impatient."

A chorus of whistling and jeering broke out from the assembled men. Then Owain stepped forward, one hand clasped upon his spear. "We will not give hostages. We will not prepare them. My ancestor, Cenau son of Coel would have faced torture gladly rather than pay a single man as hostage!"

A great shout and a banging of shields rose up from the men and Urien, his voice booming out above the uproar, roared, "If we must fight for our kindred, so be it! Let us raise our line above the mountain! Let us hold our faces above the edge! Let us raise spears above our heads and fight the Flamebearer and all his hosts! Let us kill him and his company beneath the Elmwood!"

The envoys scuttled off at this.

I strode over to the side of Urien. "So this is it then?"

"Yes harper, this is it. I hope you have a fine tune in the making, for it shall be a fine fight."

Indeed it was a fine fight. The men of Rheged rode down upon the heathen like the wind. Cloaks were flying, spears glistening, battle cries sounding, horses rearing up, and Owain driving straight into the Angle host. The Flamebearer could not hope to hold his line. I saw him, swinging his sword above his head, while Owain bore down upon him. The horse reared; with a cry Owain raised his spear high above his head. The

Flamebearer swung his sword behind his shoulder. Owain rammed his iron tipped spear down into the heathen king's throat. It was as easy as easy as sleeping for the young warrior.

It was his finest hour. The men of Bernicia were put to flight and the greatest enemy of his people was slain at his hand. But it was not just his victory but the victory of the North. As Owain had proudly stated we were not a people to be intimidated. We were still alive. The flame of our Island had not died out. Rheged and its Lord still stood defiantly in the face of the enemy. And on that night I too began to dream that we would stand, even though all else fail.

Alas that it was not to be!

I heard a cry of anguish coming from my son's cottage. Next to me Brice shifted. I felt Edryd go tense beside me. I put my hand on his shoulder. The bard opened one eye.

"She'll be alright," I whispered in my son's ear.

Carranog gave us a wink.

The bard continued.

"Urien was betrayed by the Britons, his own people. While besieging the enemy a jealous enemy had him struck down. And that was the end of my Lord.

Owain his son, who had slain the Flamebearer, returned to Rheged. But even he could not stem the tide of opposition that arose against him from his neighbours. He too fell, as did many of his brothers. Then your king Llywarch, cousin of Urien, ventured north, but he too was unable to secure the kingdom.

Now I am left. Taliesin, who was once the greatest bard in all the island. Left to look back on a sunset of heroes and kings, staring ahead into a starless night, weeping for what was and shall never be again. I stood there in high midday at the Flamebearer's fall and I have stood in the cold night at the burnt-out court of Urien. This island of the mighty shall be overrun by the heathen. Our mighty men shall vanish away into song. Truly this shall be the long sunset. But what a glorious sunset it was!"

And with that Taliesin sat down and stared into the flames of the dying fire.

I felt Edryd stir beside me. He made to get up.

"Wait, son."

Penwyn, my wife's brother spoke up to Taliesin. "Is there then no hope for the Britons?"

"With the kings fallen and the heathen creeping in, I can see no hope," came the response.

In my heart I whispered, "Yet my son's wife is of that same people." But I held my peace.

Just then the doors burst open, and my wife, dark against the night sky appeared.

Edryd leapt to his feet. "Is all well?" he cried.

My wife nodded, "Eanfled has borne you a healthy man child this very hour."

A cry of rejoicing went up from around the hall and Edryd strode beaming out the door.

Later, when all the others had gone to their sleep, I went into my son's cottage to see the babe. He was lying fast asleep in Eanfled's arms while Edryd looked on adoringly.

"What is he to be called?" I asked.

"Ardan," was his mother's reply.

I thought aloud. "The name means high hopes."

"Yes," said Edryd, "for that is what we have."

I smiled and went to my cottage.

The sun rose bold and strong the next morning. Taliesin saddled his pony and rode out while the settlement looked on and waved. Edryd proudly held the first child born to British and Anglish parents in the settlement. I sighed. Heroes might fall, but babes would be born, and sunset ever brought sunrise.

DELETERIOUS
Elise Swain
Belfast Royal Academy, Northern Ireland

Shortlisted

Ma always told me I was born in the 'Baby Bust', but the only thing I've ever seen bust in my lifetime was the buildings and my people. Shredded to pieces by searing shrapnel, explosives left under cars and in duffle bags, lingering around the country like a bad smell.

The Troubles have been hanging over us for years now, and of course, I had to be born right in the middle of it all. Just my luck! Ma and Granny Margaret have lived through it all, dear bless them; they need blessing, them pair!

The Troubles certainly are troubling; we should all be able to live without the worry of being asked what school we go to, as we innocently play on the swings.

Granny Margaret says we're going to Groomsport this weekend, so, basically that means we're going to sit in the caravan and pretend Granda Eddie didn't just die of cancer. We like to pretend in this family, pretend like Uncle Trevor only drinks with 'the boys'. He's not involved! Oh no! Not at all! Uncle Trevor would never organise gunmen. See, I'll tell you this now. Uncle Trevor is in a big organisation, so he is. We all know he is, but you can't say anything, because at the end of the day, you're already a target for the other side, but once they know you're related to someone involved, you've had it.

I'm Protestant, so I am. So Ma says I am. I never got religion. I really don't care if I walk on the Catholic side of the road or whether my eyebrows are too close for a Protestant girl.

It's a Sunday in March 1993; the view from the caravan is beautiful. The luscious green grass sways back and forth in the soothing spring breeze. Ma said she fancies a trip down into Bangor, so she dragged me into my Sunday best, which was far from my best, and away we went down to the town. I can clearly see that the inhabitants of this upper-class town have been at church 'doing their bit'. In the midst of all this hostility, how can you find such strength to pray?

Anyways, Ma took me into the chippy and I came out beaming. Strolling down the footpath with a poke of chips in one hand and a bag of yellowman in the other, we headed back up towards Main Street. It was the best day of the past few months considering Granda Eddie had just died, but little did I know it was the beginning of a miserable life for me.

Our ears were ringing after five hundred pounds of semtex sent the car it was hidden in flying through the air. The woeful wailing of the bystanders drowned out the painful calls of the victims losing blood, second by second, litre by litre. The bellows of cloud swarmed us like a pride of lions pursuing a zebra. Everything became stuck in time...

Ma ran towards the blast, probably looking for a way to help, she was a nurse in the Royal you know. People had become so accustomed to these tragedies that they were no longer afraid but knew what to do. Granny Margaret shuffled towards the gruelling travesty, shouting, "Right love, 'mon on up to help with Ma!" As I wearily made my way towards the rubble I saw Ma holding her coat over some man's arm, the beige was no longer visible, a more vibrant red colour was now on show. "Right Heather, put your hands here." Ma quivered. I looked around me, feeling my breath leave me shallowly, watching people run towards us all. I was holding onto an RUC officer's arm. He looked frail, with a tinge of death. He pointed towards Ma repeatedly saying, "Are they ok?" but I couldn't figure out the meaning of his words. I gazed down at his hand pointed towards Ma. It finally dawned on me what the man was meaning; three other officers lay spread apart on the ground shaking and screaming. My heart sank as I realised this attack incorporated more than one life in its hands. I kept the pressure on the man's arm and the commotion of the day continued. As people stood on the sidelines watching on towards the scene they realised they were in danger, "Move! Out of the road now!" Pieces of the surrounding churches were crumbling off and onto the footpath; it was like a bad omen to show that The Troubles were a long way off ending. Three million pounds in damage down the drain, and for what? So the Republicans could bring 'Freedom to Ireland', which I hasten to add didn't need freeing in the first place. My stomach twisted as I watched the officers being carted off in the back of ambulances, I had a feeling the four injuries would turn into four coffins by the end of the day.

I cried myself to sleep that night, wondering... Was I going to be next? Was the IRA personally going to murder Ma and me now? At the end of the day, maybe they already knew our connections to Uncle Trevor or saw us helping the RUC officers. Did Uncle Trevor even care about protecting us or was it all for a personal gain of being the big 'I am!'

Ma got a rap on the door from Uncle Trevor; he had information on the officers. I heard her talking to him in the scullery, it was 4am. I crept down the stairs but I was no match for Uncle Trevor's bat ears. "Well kid, they're all dead on so they are. Now away back to bed now, I'm away anyway."

"Righteo, Uncle Trevor." I was moping as I got to the banister, as I crawled back into bed, and as I fell asleep. I didn't know how the officers would move on, living with those pictures in their minds. I certainly didn't know how I was going to myself.

Ma opened my curtains, "Right Heather love, this is all a bit ridiculous. I've been calling you for the last ten minutes, now get up outta yer pit or you'll not see daylight again!"

That's just what I wanted to hear, I wanted to languish in the depths of my bedroom and never leave again. In fact, I wanted to die, so I did. I had visions of me walking out the front door and not coming home again because the IRA had kneecapped me and left me for dead.

"Right Heather love, move it now or you'll not get over in time for first bell."

I put on my uniform and sprinted up the road to school. The whole day was a blur. Everyone had seen Ma on TV being interviewed about yesterday's bombing and I could hear them muttering about how I was 'putting on the waterworks' and that 'no one died so, what was the big hassle?'

I left school early that day and never went back, much to Ma's disgust. For the next seven months my mood swings got worse and my social life ceased to exist. During those seven months four major IRA attacks took place. All turning me into more of a mess. I knew that two of these attacks took place in England, but it wasn't really all that far away and it still involved British people like me. The other one was in Newtownards where the bomb was three times as big as the one I had witnessed. The UK, but especially Northern Ireland, was a scary place and there was nothing I could do to save my country from its self-inflicted war.

On the 23rd of October, Ma had had enough of me staying indoors and forced me out with her to do some shopping. She said it would "do you the power of good, love". Ma and Granny Margaret got me a pastie from Beattie's with plenty of salt and vinegar on it, because that's the Northern Irish way, so it is! They then trailed me into Jackie Phillips' fruit shop, where I found myself dipping the dregs of the batter into the pile of salt.

"Right love, what can I get you?"

"Just six golden delicious and half a melon love."

Still to this day I wonder why Northern Irish people have a compulsion to call everyone 'love'?

Ma walked me out of the shop to cross the road towards Granny Margaret who was talking to the West Kirk's minister. She was an extremely religious woman, you know, well, when it suited her. The smell of Frizzel's fish shop was enticing. I love crab sticks and I had nearly forgotten to remind Ma to buy me a few to share with Uncle Trevor, he loved them too!

"Ma, remember you have to get some of those crab sticks for Uncle Trevor and me."

Much to my disappointment, Ma was not too happy about my request. "Heather love, until you start going back to school or get a job, you won't be getting any crab sticks. Now stop your whining or I'll give you something to whine about."

There were a few awkward stares from the minister before he gave me twenty pence to go buy two crab sticks. I saw what looked like two fishmongers delivering, well, fish. I thought to myself, 'Fresh crab sticks!' So I turned on my heels to run towards the shop...

BOOM!

The noise grounded me to the spot and the vibration knocked me onto my hunkers. Ma came running out of the church hallway screaming my name hysterically. The ringing sound was worse than that time in Bangor. As I sat on the kerb, adrenaline pumping, I looked up the road towards the lingering smoke and cries for help and I couldn't believe it. The place where I was just talking about was no longer standing, the structure impaling through many family friends and passers-by. I dreaded the thought of who was buried under it. Then I looked down at myself. A piece of wood had ripped through my side and I keeled over.

The next thing I knew I was in the back of an ambulance. A man came running up to the back of the ambulance and handed the paramedic a paper bag.

"What's this?" The paramedic was so confused, he was trying to rush me and as many others as he could get in the back of the ambulance to the hospital.

"Mate, it's some limbs, and all that we could scoop up."

I was rushed straight into surgery to stop the bleeding and when I woke up three days later Ma was at my bedside.

"Love, you're very lucky, so you are." She broke down in tears and her cheap mascara ran down her face.

"Ma what are you talking about?"

She continued to cry and then she told me. "Wilma, John, Sharon, George, Gillian... Michael, Michelle, Evelyn and Leanne; they're all gone, dead, passed on, whatever you want to call it."

I was beside myself. That could've been me. Even at that it was people who I had known for years - in fact, I had even gone to primary school with Leanne - and now they were dead and all because the IRA's bomb detonated too early.

I lay in the hospital bed staring out the window. Hoping for a day when I could do to the other side what they had done to me and my people, filling up with hatred from head to toe. I thought about all the innocent lives lost on both sides of the divide. Then I knew that I was being like the rest of this country and I didn't like that.

You see, violence will get you nowhere in life, it only leads to unnecessary death.

VIVE LA REVOLUTION
Jack Tickner
Sturminster Newton, Dorset

Shortlisted

14th July 1789, Versailles

My mother ties the laces on my silk cape, beautifully embroidered with gold stitches, like when I go riding in the mornings. I wear my thick leather riding boots, so that I don't rub my pale skin on my pony's bristly coat. My mother says I am very delicate, that I must protect myself from catching a sniffle or a cold. But today we are not going out riding, it is midnight.

The queen Marie sobs into her handkerchief and kisses my mother goodbye, they embrace in a lingering hug.

'Who will be such a great governess to the children?' the queen asks sadly.

'I have found someone,' my mother, the duchess of Polignac, reassures her dearest confidante.

'And who will be such a kind friend to me?' the queen murmurs, sorrowfully.

My mother puts her finger to the queen's lips, as she would the dauphin when he is upset. 'Shush, we will write, and when all of this is over I will return.'

We all know what *'this'* means… the revolution. We hate to say it. I had not known what a revolution was until last month, when my tutor had given me a task to find out the meaning of it and I did: *a forcible overthrow of a government or social order, in favour of a new system.*

It wasn't hard to find, since if you ventured outside the gates of Versailles you'll find the real world in the midst of a so-called revolution. A revolution is damn miserable; like Paris society; like the hungry Frenchmen; like the king and queen whose hair drained to white after the storming of the Bastille.

My sister, Aglae (who is nineteen) holds my small hand; she holds her round belly anxiously knowing any minute she will burst and add another addition to the growing Polignac family. I watch over the little Angelique, my niece, as she tumbles about, learning to walk the way all toddlers do; utter clumsiness.

Dauphin Louis stands behind his mother nervously. I smile at him but he frowns back, still getting used to his new title since his older brother Joseph died no more than a month ago. I know he will miss me, I have been a great companion to him, and I have over-heard Queen Marie say so numerous times.

'Oh, Jules is such a generous friend to my little Louis-Charles,' she would say to her ladies.

'Oh, they are brothers in everything but blood,' my mother would boast.

Though to be truthful Dauphin Joseph was much more fun. Joseph was just three years younger than me, compared to Louis-Charles's five. We had played chase, cards, pretend battles, so it was a great loss to me when he died aged just seven. Louis-Charles is so much more prudent, anxious, tender, scared; it seems the death of his brother has made the court over-protective of him. He is as pale as porridge, always first to be out of breath, no joy in his dark brown eyes. God bless his glum soul when I am gone.

My father turns to the glass door leading to the west courtyard. 'We must go now!'

My mother turns to her fidus Achates. 'Stay safe, my lady.'

'How can I be?' the queen asks, dumbfounded with grief. 'France is a hungry country!'

'Let them eat cake!' My mother chuckles sarcastically, making humour of these rotten times.

'Let them eat cake,' the queen repeats, 'yes, that's right, let them eat cake.' She raises her voice. 'Let them eat cake!' Her broad Austrian accent squeals in her brief moment of humour.

My mother turns from the queen, to the courtyard where a small carriage awaits us; two fat grey ponies are well fed and ready to make the journey. The starry sky twinkles above us. The palace of Versailles, normally bubbling with laughter, is completely silent tonight.

The carriage is plain, no comfy cushioning on the seats or silk curtains on the windows; we have to camouflage ourselves to make it out of France. My mother is first to get in, her plain blue dress looks unusually boring on her, and then it is my father, who chews on his pipe with anxiety.

'Wait!' whispers Aglae and she jerks my arm back, 'you won't get to Austria in that!' She unties my cape, ruffles up my combed black hair, and she rubs her fingers on the ground so that they are dirty and then she wipes the muck on my face, making me look like any ordinary Parisian scoundrel.

'Where are we going?' I sit in the carriage and cuddle Aglae's large belly.

'Austria.' My sister strokes my thick hair, 'Austria, Jules.'

Paris is a hellhole; the cobbles are stained with a mix of tanning and sewage, and the scent of revolution is in the air. We arrive at Paris by dawn after a long night. The five of us, mother, father, Aglae, Angelique and myself, sit huddled together alongside three gigantic suitcases, packed with the necessities we'll need to make it to Austria.

The people's faces are grotty and dishevelled, their clothes are baggy round their bony structures and their teeth are brown with decay. They stare wickedly as the carriage goes past, some curse at us or spit on the ground, others run at our carriage begging for food.

'Shall we give them some bread?' I ask. As we get deeper into Paris, further away from our pompous home at Versailles, I start to see really how bad life is in Paris compared to the life of luxury and naivety I am accustomed to.

'No!' Father hisses spitefully. 'If we give those skeletons anything then they will all come to us. They will topple this carriage over a loaf of bread!'

I look back out the carriage window, at the exhausted faces in the street. They look tired, like they are growing impatient.

'Well then, do you have anything?' they ask boldly. I doubt they will take no for an answer. I feel my mother grip my hand, only last week another aristocratic family attempting to escape France ended the day slaughtered like cattle on a farm.

'Let's just give them a little bit,' Aglae says sympathetically.

I look back at Father; he is petrified. 'You fool, they will topple our carriage!' he mutters nervously.

Mother sighs and sticks her head out the window. 'Vive la revolution!' she cries and her voice echoes through the streets of Paris. 'Vive la revolution!' Everyone in Paris replies with an over-whelming enthusiasm, as if it were a battle cry or the last words anyone will ever speak. The begging and harassment suddenly come to a halt and everyone gets back to their own business, as if we never existed.

'You must remember that,' mother says, 'it may save your life.'

'Vive la revolution,' I repeat quietly. Those three words will follow us to Austria and when (or if) we return they will be fresh in our minds; these hungry days will haunt France, years after I am gone.

C'EST LA VIE
Tiphaine Tsatsaris
London

Shortlisted

It was glowing. My eyes were trapped staring at the gold star on Father's coat as the four letters J-U-I-F had been neatly embroidered with a green thread. My parents kept repeating what a shame it was to wear it every single time we went out, but I didn't agree: I thought it made us special. It had to make us special because whenever I walked past someone, they turned around with a sorrowful, worried or even nasty look and I smiled because I knew that they were jealous. Anyway, I never went out; Ma won't let me as she says it's dangerous.

I shortly realised that Father was calling me as I looked at my left and there he was, waiting for an answer. I calmly said, "Yes?"

He quickly responded, "Finally! You haven't even touched your plate! That little ungrateful child!"

Sometimes I wish I could just ask him, "Why are you always so angry?" But I never did.

Yet my parents quickly forgot about me as Ma turned to father. "Please Pierre, you know that David will go away to Marseille tomorrow and-"

"I'm going to Marseille?"

Both of my parents looked at me with huge, round, guilty eyes. Ma started, "Oh David! You know we're not safe here. Those Boches are taking over and Marseille is so much more peaceful than Paris. And besides, it's only temporary."

"What is it that is so dangerous?! Is it the star? What does it mean? Tell me! What about Uncle Frank?" The words came out like a hammer banging her heart.

Father was enraged. "Don't you dare use that tone with me, boy! You know perfectly well that Uncle Frank left us and chose that Pétain over us! Now go to your room!"

Ma tried to stop me but I raced up to my bed where I lay, closed my eyes and frowned. Marseille?

I woke up the next morning with puffy eyes and went downstairs to eat breakfast but before entering the kitchen, I looked through the ajar door and saw Ma weeping as she listened to the radio. ...*10th of August here and it has been less than a month since the massive roundup organised by the Nazi Party and the Gestapo in our beautiful capital that is Paris. 13,152 Jews were deported and nobody knows where they are, or whether they are alive...* I violently opened the door and said, "Is this why I'm going?" Silence pervaded the room, and I took my breakfast.

As long as I can remember, Ma had always worn make-up but that day she didn't. She was struggling to close my small leather suitcase and as I watched closely, I saw two dark crescent moons under her deep blue eyes. Her hair was a mess and her hands were dry and cracked. For the first time in my life, I realised she was exhausted.

"Ma, it's okay, I'll close it."

She looked down and took a deep breath.

"Ma?"

She exhaled and smiled. "Sure mon chou, that would be great."

I leaned down and closed the suitcase, but I couldn't stop thinking about that smile. Because of me, Ma had learned how to fake it.

We had finally arrived at the train station after a long walking trip of silence and remorse. Ma turned to me and I suddenly saw that something wasn't right.

I said, "What is it?"

But as she couldn't take it anymore she burst out laughing and showed me what she was hiding - a chocolate bar! My favourite! I jumped to her neck and hugged her, but it wasn't just for the chocolate bar, it was for everything. I could smell her old Chanel perfume she always wore as I squeezed her more.

I whispered, "Thank you."

She put me down and said, "I know you never had the chance to eat one lately, but you know we couldn't afford it..."

"I know Ma, I know." For a moment we just stared at each other and

I wished it could have lasted longer but the shrill voice of the old man announcing the train departure echoed throughout the whole train station and I looked down. Ma sniffed as if to forbid the tears from showing themselves, another thing I loved about Ma.

"Well, I guess I should be going…"

I wanted to slap me for what I had just said. But it was done, and I wish I would have hugged her one last time. Because I never got the chance to do that again.

There was only one seat left. It was opposite a girl. She seemed my age, maybe a little older. She wore a long navy-blue dress, but she wasn't paying much attention to me as she was writing something inside her notebook. I sat and looked at her for a long time. Her intense green eyes were focused on the paper as she was hiding from me what she was writing. Girls… They were all the same, writing secrets inside their diary.

I finally said, "Hey."

She looked up. "What d'you want?"

"Nothing, I was just trying to make conversation. What's your name?"

She continued writing but answered, "Lucie. Do you care?"

I felt an odd mix of melancholy, resentment and anger as I burst out, "Well actually I do care because guess what? You're next to me, so you're gonna have to deal with me. Plus, we don't know for how long we're going to be stuck in that Middleofnowhere Marseille so if we stay here for the rest of our lonely lives, we're going to stick up for each other. At least I will."

She closed her book as she turned her whole body towards me. "And I will too." I knew it. It was Lucie and me against the world.

"Hey! Anything we just said there will stay a secret! Promise," I promised.

In a few hours, Lucie and I knew each other better than Father would ever know me. She hated strawberries, adored chocolate bars and had a smaller brother who didn't take the train. She was only a few months older than me, but I didn't care. Lucie laid her head on my shoulder as I asked, "What was that for?"

"Being such a good best friend."

"But I only know you for three hours."

She didn't respond.

I only said, "You're an enigma, Lucie."

Suddenly, a group of five people rushed inside the train. They wore long coats with a leather belt just over the hips.

Lucie hissed, "It's the Gestapo! Don't. Make. A. Sound. Don't talk to them. If they ask you questions, you look down."

I looked down as I saw them at the corner of my eye. They were walking slowly along the corridor between the seats. Head up, they marched straight and spread a feeling of power over us. I felt scared to breathe but they were gone now to the cabin where all the staff of the train were. I turned to Lucie, and, for the first time, I saw that she was scared.

Nobody talked for a long time. Even the eight-year-olds in front of us stopped shouting about how many teddy bears they had at home. Home. I instantly thought about Ma. Where was she? What if there had been a bombing? What if she was dead? No. I had to stop thinking about that. I had to grow up.

"Is this what it's like to grow up? Going away? Leaving everything and having to not cry about it? Lucie?"

She didn't respond, she didn't even look at me. She was watching the gold ball slowly going to sleep as it left place to its sister the Moon.

"Lucie? What is it?"

She looked back at me and laid her head back on my shoulder. "La vie, David, c'est la vie."

LADYBIRD, LADYBIRD
Lili Winstanley-Channer
London

Shortlisted

Author's note

The discovery of a fascinating possible meaning of the nursery rhyme **Ladybird, Ladybird** *inspired me to write this story about the English Reformation. The stories of such figures as Richard Gwyn captured my imagination because they are examples of the tragedy of religious intolerance that is still very topical today, and because they open up all kinds of questions about what we value the most in life and death.*

Ladybird, ladybird fly away home,

Your house is on fire and your children are gone,

All except one,

And her name is Nan,

And she hid under the baking pan.

When, on a fresh June morning, I caught a glimpse of Our Lady's bird like a tiny red jewel in the wet grass, I couldn't help smiling. We had always been taught that she belonged to Our Lady and that she would bring us luck, but it was the creature's way of coming into view so suddenly that made me feel as though I had received an unexpected gift. It was with a blithe heart that I made my way to church that morning.

Since childhood I had always been gladdened by Sunday mass. It was the sense of quiet reverence that fell on us all as we entered the church, as though the past generations who had worshipped there had left a lingering feeling of prayer, and I would slip into our pew knowing I was surrounded by the vestiges of their devotion. The images inside the church were simple and rustic enough, for we were a small country parish, but somehow they always managed to fill me with wonder, perhaps because they signalled to me that I was in the presence of something I could never fully understand. My eyes would trace the scenes in the stained-glass windows as a foreigner would a city of domes and pinnacles and flaring colour where people spoke in an exotic and beguiling tongue. I marvelled at their brightness as the sun glinted through them, enjoying the idea of the meaning they must hold without attempting to penetrate it. I would listen in the same way to the priest praying in Latin, letting the rhythmic chanting work its spell on me and feeling the thrill of hearing words that seemed to take me back to an earlier time, a time when life was lived on a grander scale. It's a curious thing that their almost mythic potency lay chiefly in the fact that I could not understand them.

From the days I was led in there by the hand I had come to lean on the solace that the Sunday service gave me, so when I noticed the changes beginning to take place in the church (on the King's orders, everyone said) I naturally felt as though the ground was shaking beneath me. Week by week I watched the objects that had fascinated me disappear, and I had an uncomfortable, squirming sense that I must resist. My heart always went out to the downtrodden. When Father Ashmall was made to leave our church, I felt the same feeling of bitter resentment against the invisible king as I always did against my father when I saw him punish one of my wayward brothers. The changes did not seem to mark the world around me as they did my mind, and years passed in the ordinary way in our community. I, however, could not go to church in the same frame of mind; I was unsettled by the absence of the face of the Virgin Mother where she had used to look down on me, and wondered why I had been stripped of my source of protection.

I started off with this muddy pool of resentful emotions but bit by bit, as I baked and weaved and sewed, it began to form into ideas, just as the beeswax ran from my pan into the moulds and took shape there as candles that could give light and smelt of honey. I was a Catholic, not a Protestant, and I resolved to steal away from our family one Sunday and find the glade in the woods where Father Ashmall was known to hold a clandestine mass every week. It was the excitement of it that fed me at first, the thrill of rebellion and secrecy, but soon I began to see something brilliant in the sight of the few of us who would be there on a wet morning, sharing our devotion under the dripping branches. I noticed the woods then in a way I never had before; I watched the first leaves bud at the beginning of spring as the words "pro nobis Christum exora" resounded in my head. I bit into the body of Christ sometimes to the sound of blackbirds' song, other times with frost in my hair or huddled in my cloak as a gale howled.

One Sunday morning when the waxing summer was at her lushest and most lavish, with foxgloves and cow parsley growing tall and thick on the waysides, I was turning to make my way down the now familiar path when my brother Roger grabbed me by the wrist and pulled me back.

'You're heading for trouble, Nan,' he told me.

A vague image of St. Catherine, straight and indomitable, addressing the crowds in Egypt, came into my mind, and I pulled my arm away. For the moment, Roger's intervention did nothing but give me the thrill of a martyr, and I gloried in walking firmly away from him. But my cocksure self-righteousness dried up with the morning dew, while his words lingered in my mind. By the time I brushed through the thick green foliage into our glade I was remembering the stories we had heard of priests only parishes away being hunted out and arrested. As the weeks passed the numbers of our small group dwindled, and in my mind's eye I saw the authorities closing in on us like wolves. But the more unjust, the more ferocious I pictured them, the more I was certain I was in the right and the more strongly I felt my duty of loyalty to Father Ashmall. However hunted, however persecuted we were, if all the rest of the flock deserted our cause, I would be there.

One day I stumbled across our priest sitting at the foot of a great beech tree. I greeted him in the ordinary way, although there was something terribly wrong in the sight of him sitting in the damp moss, looking to me hardly more alive than a cold and grey boulder or tree stump.

'The sheriff will be here tomorrow, Nan,' he said. 'The whole village knows where we meet – I will be taken.'

I could barely get the words out of my mouth, but gulped something about hiding in the woods.

He shook his head. 'My dearest friend, whom I studied with, was taken to Tyburn. He was hung, drawn and quartered – the punishment for treason. It isn't only Roman Catholics being executed there, but Protestant recusants, too – burnt for heresy. I don't know who is right and who is wrong in this, Nan, but the whole country is going up in flames. I don't see much Christianity in this anywhere. Right or wrong, I have chosen to stand by the faith I was brought up in, and I must stand by it to the last, and go where my brethren have gone. But you, you don't need to make enemies out of the Protestants any longer. That isn't the way to create a land where all will be able to worship where they feel they are led.'

I looked down and saw a ladybird on my right hand, red and ruby-like.

THE SOLDIER'S CIVIL WAR
Lucas Yates
Bancroft's School, Woodford Green, Essex

Shortlisted

In 1861 two sides were forged.

One fighting for the good of others, the other fighting for the good of themselves.

South Carolina was the first to go, those dirty scums. They wanted slavery to continue, they thought it was okay. Being locked up, forced to do hard labour. I don't see how anyone could think that that was okay. Other states had seceded from our great nation and now they practically had an army lying in wait for the right moment. Abraham stuck with our side, General Lee was our enemy. And so it started.

I didn't want to fight. Didn't really have a choice. I was never the aggressive type when I was younger, or when I went to war. But none of that mattered. As long as they had men nothing else mattered. Generals saw them as faceless figures. I saw them as friends, friends who I would inevitably lose through bloodshed or killing. Lives are so fragile, so very easily taken away.

"Oi! Johnny!" exclaimed Frank, looking drunk as usual. He hobbled along towards me, his brown tattered shoes squelching in the deep, moist mud. "Boss is lettin' us have one more round o' whisky, sure you don't wanna join us?"

"No Frank, you have it." I stared back into my journal. Day 37. 'How much more?' I thought to myself. A soft, warm sun touched the curve of the earth, almost resting after a long day. I wish I had something like that, somewhere safe, somewhere I can feel at home.

"Attention!"

Everyone stood up strong and bold. I stumbled up to my feet.

The General gave me a nasty stare. "Do it right soldier John or you'll be doing it a thousand more times!" he shouted, his grey mouse-like moustache moving whenever he talked, almost as if it were alive. "Tomorrow is going to be a special day. Tomorrow we beat our enemies! We all have a job to do boys, and if anybody doesn't do theirs, they'll be handed to the Confederates. Do I make myself clear?"

"Yes sir!" everyone shouted.

I kept my mouth shut.

He turned to look at me again with that same glint of hatred still lingering in his eyes. "I said do I make myself clear!"

Everyone turned to look at me.

There was a long pause while I thought whether to answer or to shove his teeth through his skull. I wasn't strong enough. "Yes sir," I mumbled.

"Just as I thought." He glowered. "Load your rifles, sharpen your bayonets. Tomorrow there's a war to be won!"

Last night's sleep was horrible yet no different to any other, and here we were, creeping silently through the forest, like wild animals on the hunt. Nothing stirred. The silence was deafening in my ears, only the beating of my own heart could be heard. The misty fog curled around the trees, as though being enticed towards them. A big willow tree stood tall above the rest, its arms branching down trying to reach the ground.

I looked at the men around me, men who had given up their families to help end this war. I could feel the drops of dew, from the moist grass, dripping down my ankles through my ragged socks, ripped from the past days of fighting.

I wandered away from the group. The dense forest blocked out the morning light. Suddenly I heard a snap of a twig. I froze. My senses on full alert. No-one from the Union was here. Only me. I crept forward. Slowly. Cautiously. I peered round a huge fir tree. There, in the clearing, were two men lighting a cigarette, taking a drag. South Carolina. The accent was definitely from South Carolina. I started panting, my heart skipping several beats. 'They prepared me for this,' I told myself. I gulped. I stood out from the safety of the tree.

"Don't move!" I exclaimed, my rifle held out in front of me, trying to sound as confident as I possibly could, but the two men were already on me. The cigarettes lay there on the ground, smoke, drifting up to the already hazy fog. A loaded gun was pointing towards me. My heart filled with dread but my instinct took over. I pulled the trigger. The boy stumbled to the floor his legs buckling from under him, a single stream of blood ran slowly down his chest. His friend, horrified by what he had witnessed dropped his weapon and rushed to help him.

'What have I done?' I thought to myself. "They could have been friends in another life." The gunshot attracted everyone's attention, from both sides of the fence. Guns were fired. Lives were taken. The Battle of Shiloh had begun.

Ruby light came from every direction as grenades exploded on impact. Shrapnel flew like throwing knives across the open graveyard that was the battlefield. Earth erupted as bullets peppered the air. It was a volcano of colour. Men were falling either side of me, faces that I recognised were just shadows of the life that had existed there. I was at the tatty torn edge of the earth. It was too much to take in.

"Hold your ground!" screamed the general through the devastation. Even his stern face was filled with desperation. Men fled the battle, trying to run from the chaos. I was tempted to join them but my conscience kept me in the fight. Then, the earth exploded from under me. I was in the air. Time had slowed. I was weightless, drifting. This was it. I could feel it. Gravity took hold of me again. I hit the ground hard. The wind was suddenly knocked out of me. I could feel myself losing consciousness. The world had become a blur and faded away as my eyes shut.

It was dark when I woke up. There were no stars in the sky. The rising smoke made sure of that. An acrid smell of gunpowder filled the air. A gashing wound on my leg throbbed with pain. All around me the dead lay scattered. Limbs and body parts were flung from the impact of explosion. My mind was buzzing, unsure whether I was dead or alive. As I looked around, anyone that was still breathing had a luminous substance spread over their wounds. It was unrecognisable to me. The same thing was in my leg wound, like paint spreading over a wet canvas. On a normal day I would have been curious, I would have been afraid, but I was too tired to worry. If the explosion didn't kill me, that most likely would. My head took over and I fell back to sleep.

"Wake up soldier." That voice, it sounded familiar, but more human, more empathetic. "Do what your General says when he's talking to you!"

"What?" I asked, still very drowsy. It was the General, that mouse still attached to his upper lip.

"Ah, you're awake! Guess what, soldier, we won, the last of them were killed off late last night." He tried helping me to my feet. "Easy, easy," he said. "You're not strong enough."

This was the nicest I had ever seen the General. "General, what is this thing on my leg?" I asked.

"Oh that, son, is going to make you heal a whole lot quicker." Listening to the General came the flooding realisation that I would be back in the killing fields much sooner than I'd hoped.

My war was not over.